A DAD-SIZED
CHALLENGE

T0385487

A DAD-SIZED CHALLENGE

Building a Life-Changing Relationship with Your Son

JEFF KINLEY

Kregel
Publications

A Dad-Sized Challenge: Building a Life-Changing Relationship with Your Son

© 2009 by Jeff Kinley

Published by Kregel Publications, a division of Kregel, Inc., P.O. Box 2607, Grand Rapids, MI 49501.

Library of Congress Cataloging-in-Publication Data
Kinley, Jeff.
  A dad-sized challenge : building a life-changing relationship with your son / Jeff Kinley.
    p. cm.
Includes bibliographical references.
1. Fathers—Religious life. 2. Fathers and sons—Religious aspects—Christianity. I. Title.
BV4529.17.K56   2009   248.8'421—dc22   2009001487

ISBN 978-0-8254-2949-1

Printed in the United States of America
09 10 11 12 13 / 5 4 3 2 1

Gratefully dedicated to my dad,
J. B. Kinley,
who taught me how to be a man

Contents

Introduction

In our gender-neutral society, a man's place in the world seems to be shrinking. So much so that anything "just for males" is frowned upon, and often labeled as sexist.

What's going on here? Has the world gone mad? Isn't there anywhere a man can go and be a man? And if so, where is that place? Is it the men's grill at the country club? The cigar shop? The hunting lodge? Poker night at Ted's?

Maybe.

May I suggest another place? A secret hideaway better than the clubhouse you built in the woods when you were a kid. You know, the one with the sign that read "No Girls Allowed." It's a place so unique that there's not another like it in the world. A place so personal, only you and one other person have keys to it. Its location is found in a remote area, in a secluded spot chosen by you alone.

It's a place for you and your son. Just you and your boy . . . *together*.

Rewind your memory to the day your son was born. It's a vivid scene, isn't it? With cerebral surround sound and hi-def resolution, it plays like a blockbuster movie in your brain. You've watched it over and over again. And it never gets old, does it? The proudest day of your life.

That unforgettable date is a memory that touches a part of you like nothing else, tapping into the very vein of manhood within you. You felt so complete. So fulfilled. So manly. Like you'd just nailed a last-second shot to win a national championship. You hadn't, of course. But something much better and greater had happened.

INTRODUCTION

You had a son.

Do you remember the excitement? The anticipation? The fear? The sights, sounds—and smells—of that birthing room? Do you recall how amazed you were at the pain threshold reached by your wife, and feeling put to shame by her ability to endure it . . . even with drugs? Do you remember being grateful you're not a woman? That you'd rather go to war or dig ditches the rest of your natural life than have an eight-pound human squeezed out of your body?

Then you caught the first glimpse of your son, and soon you were cradling him in your arms. Not firmly, like a signed football from Brett Favre, but gently, like a newly constructed model airplane, still afraid you might somehow break him.

He was asleep—something you soon learned to appreciate—and you stared at his face in bewilderment. In that moment the gravity of what had just happened landed squarely on your shoulders.

Holy cow! I'm a dad!

And life would never be the same.

You were overwhelmed with an odd mixture of joy, uncertainty, fear . . . and the high calling God had just laid in your lap.

You tried to figure out who he looks like. You wondered . . . will he play baseball or football? Will he be a hunter? Play guitar? Have an engineer's mind? Become an artist? Will he be naturally witty like his dad, or will he turn out to be a stick-in-the-mud like his mom's dad?

You fast-forwarded to the time the two of you would play catch, fish, or just wrestle on the living-room floor. You contemplated backpacking in the mountains, camping by the lake, fly-fishing on the river, shouting side-by-side at a college football game, attending a concert, watching a car race, hunting in the woods, or just hanging out at the local burger joint . . .

. . . *together.*

And you wondered what kind of man he'd turn out to be.

You found yourself making heartfelt promises to him. And to God. You vowed to be the father this boy deserves, his best friend in a close, manly, unbreakable bond of life. No matter what it takes.

But in spite of your sincerity, life happens, and those aspirations and promises fade like an old photograph. You turn around, and four years have passed. You blink and ten more fly by. And you wonder where the time went. You began well, but you got tired . . . and distracted. But athletes aren't remembered for how they *start* the race. Only for how they finish. And your race isn't over yet.

If you're like most dads, you still want to make good on all those promises you made in that hospital room. Pledges made as you laid him in his crib, kissing him on the cheek and placing that cheap, shiny baseball glove beside him.

Maybe you dream of having the kind of relationship you and your dad enjoyed. Or maybe you hope to be completely different from your dad. Either way, you wish for the kind of father-son relationship every man hopes for in that moment. A friendship. A bond like no other. Different from what moms have with their daughters. It's a bond only a man can know. A man and his son. And it's just for you and your boy.

Not to take anything away from girls. You can still call your daughter "princess" or "daddy's little girl." But that's another kind of relationship. Another book. And another author.

A Dad-Sized Challenge is about you and your son . . . together. It's about your relationship with him, and how the two of you build a sacred spot. A place where he realizes that if he could choose any dad in the world, it would be you every time. It's about *enjoying* your son. About reaching your potential as a father. And make no mistake about it, you *can* be a great dad. Rest assured, you're not the first man who's faced this challenge. And you're not the first to make mistakes. We all bear the bruises and scars of faulty fatherhood.

As father to a son, you're a member of a very special fraternity. And so am I. My dad was raised in a family of nine sons and one daughter, *bless her heart*—a versatile Southern phrase that here means, "I'm glad I'm not the only daughter in a house with nine sons!" All eight of my dad's brothers married and had kids. Lots of kids. But my dad had the honor of fathering three boys. Then the oldest of those boys had three sons of his own. Then *I* had three boys. As of this writing, one of my brother's sons just celebrated the arrival of son number two.

Anyone see a pattern here? Apparently, the sap in our family tree is testosterone! The good news is, of course, the Kinley name is likely to be around for centuries!

So you can see that there's quite a heritage of boys in our family. Add to this my working with teenage boys and their dads for the past twenty-six years in student ministry and it seems all my life I've been surrounded by boys—uncles, more male cousins than I can count, brothers . . . and best of all, sons.

I'm a dad. Just like you.

And as dads, you and I make up a league of ordinary men commissioned with the extraordinary task of bringing boys into manhood. Our journey is long and packed with many challenges along the way. But our destination is clear, and we never walk alone. So gear up, Dad.

Let's do this!

CHAPTER 1

Where's the *Hooah*?

I'm a big fan of castles. Always have been. I guess I like them because they conjure up images of armor-clad knights on horses and
archers perched on tower walls. I envision local lords and ladies in
smoky banquet halls, seated at rough-hewn tables, feasting on freshly
roasted Cornish hen and potatoes. I imagine dark, damp, and drafty
rooms, lit only by the flames of a huge fireplace and candles. I see
thick stone walls and wide moats. Then again, maybe I like castles
just because I'm also a big fan of *Monty Python and the Holy Grail*.

In my most recent visit to the U.K., though, my son Stuart and I
walked among what remains of one of Wales' most renowned treasures—Raglan Castle. This medieval stronghold, rising majestically
over the green Welsh countryside, was begun in the fifteenth century
by Sir William Thomas. Following Sir Thomas's death, his son continued construction work on the castle, and may have been respon-
sible for the structure's most prominent feature—the Great Tower.
This imposing, multisided ancient skyscraper, with its five-story
height and multiple gun and arrow slits, was meant to intimidate all
who approached the castle.

A few hundred years went by and Raglan passed through the
hands of a few earls before coming into the ownership of the Marquis
of Worcester—yes, pronounced like the steak sauce. This chap sup-
ported Britain's king during a time when the monarch was engaged in
a civil war with his own parliament. This conflict brought the battle
to the gates of Raglan Castle in the mid-1600s, ultimately breaching
the walls and conquering it.

And just to make sure no one ever occupied it again, parliaments' soldiers systematically began dismantling the huge structure. Ascending to the summit of the Great Tower, soldiers hammered away at the stone and masonry work. After some time, however, it became apparent that there simply weren't enough pick axes, time, or manpower to complete the Herculean task. So instead, they removed all of Raglan's wood floors, destroying anything else they could to render it unlivable. In the ensuing centuries, the castle suffered greatly, exposed to the elements, time, and the plundering of local residents.

Visit Raglan Castle today and you'll see that Great Tower exactly as those soldiers left it centuries earlier. Stuart and I made the long climb up the few hundred spiral stone steps leading to the top of that massive stone edifice. Standing there, we could see for miles in all directions, and again imagined the splendor and strength that was once mighty Raglan Castle.

Manhood as Tower

Call me sentimental, but I see a parallel between famous Raglan Castle and the nobility of manhood. Like Raglan, masculinity is, at its core, something honorable. Even majestic. Once upon a time, to be a man meant you were strong, dependable, protective, permanent. You *wanted* to be a man. It was something every young boy aspired to.

Back in the day, there used to be heroes. Remember those guys? Men to emulate and imitate. Bigger-than-life individuals whose character and deeds inspired boys to become something greater than themselves. To become *men*.

But I don't see heroes much these days. Not long ago, I asked a group of teenage boys who their heroes were. And for the next sixty seconds the only sound I heard was the grass growing outside. After some prodding, they finally began to open up. But the names of their heroes all turned out to be characters found in video games and fiction spy novels. Not one had an actual living person as their hero.

It's not surprising that manhood, like Raglan Castle, has also suffered under siege—from elements of popular culture and changing times. As a result, young men have difficulty identifying heroes and choosing whom to admire. The characteristics that once set us apart as men have slowly eroded away. Forces have waged war against manhood's impenetrable walls. Once protected and secure, the castle has been compromised. The moat of masculinity has been crossed by invading ideologies and the castle walls eroded by political correctness. As a result, few people even remember what a real man looks like. Like an old postcard, the image of manhood has faded and its worth downgraded to flea-market value.

And that's a crying shame.

So then what does it mean to be male? There are, of course, as many definitions of manhood as there are people willing to give them. And I won't even attempt a one-size-fits-all description. As men, we wouldn't want to limit our entire identity to technical terms or trendy catch phrases. After all, we're much deeper than that, aren't we? So instead, let's paint a more colorful portrait of manhood . . . and ultimately of fatherhood.

For most of my youth, my image of men came from movies and television. John Wayne, Bruce Willis, Rambo, Schwarzenegger, William Wallace, Magnum P. I., James Bond, and of course Chuck Norris. Now those guys could kick some tail. When I finally looked into—of all places—the Bible, I met some other guys who I now believe help define our image of masculinity. These men fit well into the category of *man*.

Do you recall the shepherds mentioned at Jesus' birth? As in "keeping watch over their flocks by night"? I have a hunch you and I may have something in common with those guys. I'm not talking about the men in your church's annual Christmas program. You know the guys who pose like characters in a Shakespearean play, pointing pensively to the stars and proclaiming, "Hark, what star is that in yonder sky?"

I don't think so.

Maybe their neatly trimmed beards give them away. At any rate, I suspect the original shepherd guys more closely resembled your redneck cousin Ricky and his hunting buddies. Men who spend their weekends in a remote deer stand are probably more like the original herdsmen than Deacon Jim, guilted into the shepherd role because nobody else signed up.

In reality, shepherds in Jesus' day were dirty men. Smelly critters. With scraggly beards. You know, the kind of beard that grows down the neck and migrates up onto the cheekbones. These guys had few, if any, manners. And their language was as salty as the nearby Dead Sea. Their clothes were likely torn from multiple encounters with thorn bushes. They had calloused hands, with months of gunk packed under their fingernails. Their faces displayed the effects of years exposed to the harsh Middle East sun. They knew well both the bitter cold and blistering heat that came with the job.

These were desert-men, accustomed to the hard path of life. A rough crowd for sure. And you could see it in their eyes. Notorious lowlifes and economic bottom-feeders, their reputation for lying disqualified them from testifying in a court of law. Far from the gentle, soft-skinned shepherd image so often sold to us, these rugged warriors had done battle with lions, bears, and other wild beasts.

They were probably ugly too.

But nobody likes to look at an ugly Bible character. So we reinvent our shepherds, dressing them like they just walked out of the lambs' wool section of Brooks Brothers.

I find it refreshing that God chose these scalawags to be the very first news-bearers of Jesus' birth.

Anyway, they remind me of what the average man might have been like in Jesus' time. Ordinary, everyday guys. Not an ounce of pretentiousness. No climbing up the corporate ladder, kissing up to the boss, trying to make a name for themselves. They weren't working toward a gold watch at retirement. They just wanted some hot grub at the end of the day. They were regular men—guys like us who just do our jobs and listen to some Skynyrd blaring from the truck radio.

Like cousin Ricky.

It's sad, really, what society and even the church have done to the concept of manhood. They've both bought into the lie that men are supposed to be as passive as the sheep those ancient shepherds once herded. Docile. Compliant. Obedient. Tame.

Boring.

Sorry, but I don't buy that image. And if that's what a man's supposed to be, then I'd rather be a barbarian. I'm not advocating, of course, that we swing the pendulum toward the dominating, chauvinistic, sexist, rude beast perceived by some to be the average "Christian" man. You know what I mean. This is the guy who exploits women, in the name of God of course, pressuring them into "submission," which generally means women exist to serve the whims of their men. "Their" women are often expected to stay quiet in church and without question accept the subservient role as the weaker sex.

This abuse of gender roles is a perversion of the Creator's original intention. The idea of an authentic man got twisted into the notion that "real" men should keep women, as well as other men, under their thumbs, like the ultimate bully would do. That kind of domination is a sad outgrowth of intense male insecurity, and we struggle to overcome it. But the bottom line is that the need to feel secure is merely a way to justify the oppression of others. The same motivation and outcome can be seen in drug lords, gangsters, dictators, hard-driving CEOs, and egomaniacal, empire-building preachers.

In many Christian circles, toleration of this twisted ideal has given men the license to be jerks who mistreat their wives and steamroll their children . . . especially their sons. More about this in a later discussion, but suffice it to say that this idea of manhood belittles women and, in the end, manhood itself.

All it really proves is that, left to his own inclinations, man is an ugly, selfish beast.

And are we as Christian men any different?

As the pendulum swings the other direction, some men have unfortunately embraced passivity. Particularly when it comes to taking responsibility for inspiring our sons to authentic manhood.

We have to reject these misapplications of manhood. Instead, we should admit our mistakes, cut our losses, and move on with a better understanding of our destiny as dads.

So in a world where men are considered to be either dominating ogres or passive wimps, where do we find the balance? Where do we discover the true core of masculinity? Where in all this confusion is real manhood as it was intended to be? Can you really lead your son without bullying or bruising him? Can you feel good about being a man without being thought of as a chauvinist pig? Can you freely celebrate your masculinity without feeling guilty? Can you fully embrace your manhood without feeling like you've trespassed over the boundary of political correctness? No one ever asks, "Is it okay to be a woman?" But, hey, is it really okay to be a man?

Definitely.

Think about the things that are uniquely male as opposed to female . . . aside from the obvious physical distinctions—more muscle mass, larger frame, and a penis. Other distinctives are fairly apparent, seen mostly in the emotional and psychological differences between men and women. None of these qualities are better. Just different. Very different.

Most men tend to be direct and practical, for example, while women are generally more holistic and intuitive. If you offend a guy, he'll say, "Hey, buddy, watch it!" A woman will stop speaking to you, and expect you to guess why she's mad.

A woman's appearance deteriorates—at least in her mind—during the night. We men wake up in the morning just as good-looking—at least in our minds—as we did when we went to bed.

When women are depressed, they eat or go shopping. Men hit golf balls, work on the car, or declare BB-gun wars on backyard squirrels.

Women remember important dates. Men can't remember anniversaries, but we can recall, with amazing detail, obscure major-league batting averages and the names and phone numbers of every girlfriend since the second grade.

A man's greatest weapons are our hunting rifles and our power tools. A woman's arsenal includes cosmetics and tears.

And speaking of tears. Women can find a reason to cry over just about anything, as in "I'm so happy for you, Jen," sniff, sniff. "Those shoes go with your eyes so well." Men tend to cry only during the final moments of major sports events and the climactic scenes of epic movies like *Saving Private Ryan*.

A man's pride can be found in his toys, technology, and gadgets. Women simply cannot appreciate the necessity of a fifty-two-inch plasma screen.

Women are tidy. Men, however, consider it a challenge to see how high we can stack trash in the garbage can.

Women need to be told how pretty they are. Men need a standing ovation for emptying the dishwasher.

Women stress over naming their children. Men stress over naming their cars.

Women instinctively know what to do when someone cries. At the first sign of tears, men begin looking for something in the house to repair.

Women think about risks before acting. Men think about how cool we'll look in front of our friends, and only think about risk while being sewn up in the emergency room.

Women answer questions with dissertation-like responses. Men can say all they need to communicate in a grunt or a "Mmm-hmm."

You cannot pry the remote from a man's hands, even while he's asleep.

Men don't need to ask for directions because we always know where we're going. Maps are the devil. But GPS gadgets are a built-in budget necessity.

When a women is injured, she calls out for her husband. When a man is injured, he calls out to various deities—in colorful language.

Women can remember every outfit they've worn in the past five years. Men can't remember what they wore yesterday unless we look on the bedroom floor.

Men can write their names in the snow.

I rest my case.

The point is that men are men. We are not the masculine version of women. We have our own gender. Unique. Different. Special. And that's a good thing. And what distinguishes boys from girls is seen early on in life. As young boys we enjoyed firecrackers and blowing up stuff, playing army, shooting slingshots and homemade bows and arrows, climbing trees, poking things with sticks, terrorizing the neighborhood cat just to see if it always lands on its feet. Boys enjoy pulling the dog's tail, splashing in mud puddles, finding a weird-looking bug, catching frogs, seeing a snail shrivel up under a pile of salt, playing in the rain, building our own skateboards, yelling like Tarzan on a rope swing, digging in the dirt, experimenting with household chemicals, picking at the scabs our moms told us to leave alone, playing games where guys can hit each other, sword-fighting with sticks, jumping off the garage roof or a cliff, playing with fire, BB guns, and fast cars. We enjoy video games and action movies with lots of fighting, and there must be some blood involved. We love to build things or tear them apart just to see how they work. We're naturally inquisitive. We want to *know*.

These are the kinds of things we do that make us feel like guys. They're a natural part of who we are, encoded in our DNA just as much as the peach fuzz that eventually sprouts on our chins. We have a passionate desire to know that what we *do* really matters in life. This is one reason we derive so much of our self-esteem from our jobs and careers.

But it's this same hunger for significance that also motivates us to pour our lives into our sons. Within most every dad lies the irrepressible desire to bond with his son. That desire, though stronger in some men than in others, is a part of God's character in us to naturally long for a strong relationship with our sons. That's because, deep within us, we know our sons are our noble cause. Our crowning achievement. Our legacy. Our *magnum opus*.

Our Greatest Effort

Our sons are the castles we patiently build and vigorously defend. And no matter what else we may achieve in this life—awards, recognition, position, financial security, possessions, ministries, status—nothing compares to the gallant effort we pour into our boys. Everything else in life ends up as a cheap plaque on the wall, destined one day for the attic or a garage sale. But our very *soul* lives on through our sons. They are what we fight for, what we sacrifice for, what we lay down our lives for.

Our boys do not become men by default or by happy accident. Manhood doesn't automatically or magically happen with time, growth, and age. Instead, a boy grows into a real man because a real man is there to show the way for him. Every boy needs a male role model for manhood. A mentor. And though there can, and should, be other significant men in a boy's life—coaches, youth leaders, scoutmasters, teachers—none of them can make a man out of your boy quite like you can.

Without you to show him the way in life, your son will stumble and wander aimlessly in the dark on his journey to maturity. He will flounder his way through childhood and adolescence, lost in a world of confusing ideologies and value systems. Trust me on this one. I'm not the smartest man in the galaxy, but I do try to pay attention. And over the last twenty-six years I've observed, studied, and worked with countless dads and sons. Some of the things I've seen have crushed my heart. Absent dads who sold their souls to the company while neglecting their sons. Critical, condemning fathers. Silent types who hardly communicated with their boys. Religious zealots who pressured their sons into active "Christian duty" through a daily barrage of guilt and "God's rules." Passive men who abdicated their fatherly role to their wives. Overbearing men who, because of latent insecurities, forced their sons into trying to achieve the things that the dads never accomplished. And every one of these guys thought they were teaching their sons to become real men.

Not one of them did.

What they did instead was perpetuate a myth of manhood, a facade that says men are either too tough to care or too busy with other important things. They couldn't give their sons the gift of authentic manhood because they couldn't give something they didn't personally possess. And all those boys, now grown and many with families of their own, still struggle to overcome the damage done by well-meaning, but unwise dads.

Oh, these boys eventually do become men, but most are like unguided missiles. And like those missiles, they end up self-destructing or hitting the wrong target. And the cycle continues, passed on to the next generation of sons.

A father casts a very long shadow.

Maybe you're one of those boys. The shadow of your own father may still haunt you like chronic back pain.

But I trust that you want more for your son. He deserves better, doesn't he? You want him to grow into authentic manhood. To become the man he was created to be. To fulfill his destiny as a human being.

In the pages that follow, you and I will enter into a conversation. We'll step out onto the front porch and have a man-to-man talk about our sons and ourselves. No lectures, but I'll let you in on some of the things I've observed and experienced in my years of working with dads and sons. Many of the things I've seen have helped me tremendously in my relationship with my own boys. Other things have driven me to my knees, praying, "God, please don't let me be that kind of dad."

Fatherhood is not a game, and I won't merely send in plays to you from the comfort of the sidelines, coaching with my headset and clipboard. As you already know, I'm the father of three teenage boys.

Boys.

Three of them.

All teenagers.

And this is, I'm glad to announce, without a doubt the most exciting time of my life so far. I've dreamed about this season of life since the day I first saw my wife give birth. Honestly, part of me wishes I could press "pause," freezing time so I can keep them as teenagers, and here with me just a little longer. But time marches on, doesn't it? So I'm determined to seize the day, squeezing every drop I can out of each moment with them. They grow up fast, my friend.

In my all-time favorite film, *Braveheart*, one scene hits me right in the gut. Following a brutal battle (pick any one you like), William Wallace's best friend, Hamish Campbell, is tending to his own father's wounds, and it's clear that Dad isn't going to make it. Knowing this, the elder Campbell looks into his son's eyes one last time:

CAMPBELL: I'm dying. Let me be.

HAMISH: [*with tears filling his eyes*] No. You're not going to die. You're going to live.

CAMPBELL: [*looking up to make eye contact with his son*] I've lived long enough to live free . . . and proud to see you become the man that you are . . . I'm a happy man.

Would you like to be able to say that to your son on your deathbed? That you've lived just long enough to see him become the man he was meant to be? Wow! To be so proud of your boy that even death itself can't steal your joy! I can think of nothing better. What an incredible achievement.

Dad, just like you, I'm neck-deep in the trenches of parenting. I'm in the foxhole of fatherhood with you. The same bullets whizzing past your head are whizzing past mine. We're wearing the same uniform, so let's fight our enemies together. In the pages that follow, we'll talk of great wins, but also heartbreaking losses. I'll also show you my own battle scars, revealing my faults and failures—times when I've blown it. I'll tell stories of what I believe it takes to help your son earn his stripes and become his own man.

But for that to happen, we must vow to never, ever surrender the fight. The cost of laying down our weapons is too great a price to pay. Instead, during those times when the war seems lost, we'll reload and charge forward together with a man-sized battle cry.

Are you with me?

HOOAH!

CHAPTER 2

GPS

The bags were packed. The Expedition was loaded. Sack lunches were prepared. My three boys each had their iPods fully charged and were ready for the long journey that lay ahead. We were about to leave for a weeklong trek across the country. Beginning from our home in Little Rock, the plan was to head east seven hundred miles (in one day) to South Carolina, to see my extended family. After just one day there, we'd rise early the next day and travel north to Washington, D.C., where our boys would experience the nation's capital for the first time—the Smithsonian, the White House, the Lincoln Memorial, Ford's Theater—a teenage boy's dream vacation. After a few days there, we'd drive north to New York City before arriving at our final destination—the United States Military Academy at West Point. Our oldest son, Clayton, had expressed more than a passing interest in this legendary institution, so this spring break excursion was actually a college trip in disguise.

As dad and self-appointed driver, my job was to keep us on track, on schedule, and most importantly, always moving toward our destination. But as important as my duties were, the most critical responsibility fell to my wife-navigator, Beverly. She had spent several late nights studying routes and highways, using Mapquest and Google to find the best course to our final destination. She would be our eyes. Our radar. Our travel guide—the Kinleys are still in the Stone Age with no GPS in the family SUV. By the way, you ever wonder why it's a lady's voice in that GPS? "Turn right in one hundred feet." "Now arriving at destination." Even in technology, women are still telling us which way to go. Be that as it may, we nevertheless placed the utmost confidence in Mom. After all, she's the most organized person on the planet, so it made the most sense for these directional duties to land in her lap.

The South Carolina leg of the journey went without a hitch as we'd made that trip countless times before. From Carolina to D.C. was a little more challenging, considering we were to stay with friends in nearby Arlington, Virginia, and had to weave our way through a few neighborhoods before finding their place. The trip up to the Big Apple was even more challenging, as there were several tollways and a confusing amount of road options leading into the city. Once we exited the tunnel beneath the river and emerged into Manhattan, the real fun kicked in.

Okay . . . picture a metropolis buzzing with yellow taxicabs zipping through a multilane maze of rush-hour traffic like roaches scurrying when you snap on the light. Now picture in the middle of this yellow landscape, a huge green SUV inching its way through downtown like a giant slug. It's a miracle we didn't scrape, bump, or crash into another car. I quickly figured out why people in New York take the subway, a taxi, or just walk. Actually the hard part wasn't getting into the city, but rather exiting it. Several course corrections had to be made, and some unexpected road options popped up that weren't covered on the map. Internet mapping isn't always correct. The result was that upon leaving New York I made a wrong turn and ended up in New Jersey.

Lost.

Nothing against New Jersey, but we weren't exactly prepared for a tour of residential urbanville. After several more wrong turns and an hour of driving, we stumbled on a kind soul at a gas station who led us to the right highway toward West Point. And after a few heated arguments—in which everybody blamed everybody else—Mom was officially relieved of her navigational duties by a vote of 4 to 1.

It's hard enough to endure a trip of several thousand miles battling fatigue, eye strain, lower-back pain, and boredom, and that's even when you know where you're going. But try navigating to a faraway destination you've never been to before.

That's what it's like to have a son.

Even when he's your second or third boy, it's not the same, because *he's* not the same. You can't parent boy number three in the exact same way that you did your first son. You can't just lay a generic parenting template over your relationship with him, plugging in some travel route that worked with the other boy. That's because each son requires different things from you. In other words, in this father-son journey, the map changes with each new boy. Oh, the basic principles may be the same, but because the landscape of childhood and adolescence keeps changing, so must your ability to flex and refine your parenting skills. Like a GPS, you have to continually download the updated best route to a destination called Authentic Manhood.

A Trip to the Optometrist

As dads, we have to ask ourselves, "How do I guide my boy in the right path?" To answer that question, we first have to develop vision. For most of us, however, that word sounds a bit intimidating. That's because the majority of us aren't CEOs or corporate heads—men we typically associate with great vision. After all, we're not building empires or initiating corporate advances on a national or global scale. We're busy enough just trying to make ends meet and be good dads, right? But vision isn't as elusive or unattainable as it may seem. It's something every dad can have.

When Walt Disney World opened in 1971, two upper-level executives of that vast entertainment empire were walking the park when one remarked to the other, "I sure wish Walt could have been here to see this." To which his friend quickly replied, "He *did* see it. That's why it's here."

Vision is simply the ability to see something that isn't there yet. But seeing it isn't enough. You must also have the willingness, commitment, and endurance to help bring it to pass. The good news for you and me is that corporate America doesn't have a monopoly on vision. Anyone who can dream can have vision. And nowhere is that vision more needed than in the relationship between a dad and his son.

If you've ever dreamed of having a strong bond with your son, then you're already on the right path. Vision is simply making your dreams come to life.

Part of my DNA dictated that I inherit poor eyesight. To be specific, nearsightedness. And if you've ever been to the eye doctor, you're probably familiar with those eye charts—you know, the ones on the wall with the different sized letters? Some are big and easy to see while others are almost microscopic. And depending on your vision, some or all may be out of focus. Recently I've had to use reading glasses to help me clearly see things like my computer screen, newspapers, and books. A sign of age, I suppose.

Regardless, knowing this would be my future, I determined not to be that dad with the granny glasses perpetually resting on the end of his nose. I didn't want to spend the rest of my life peering over the tops of those sad things. So I opted instead for the nerdiest pair of reading glasses I could find. Now, instead of looking like granny, I'm a little more Clark Kent. Not long ago, an eye surgeon friend of mine offered to perform LASIK surgery on me free of charge, but after a consultation, it was determined that my eyes weren't good candidates for this procedure. The good news is that I can see to read, and the "nerd look" is in style again . . . at least for now.

What about you? How's your eyesight? What do you see when you see your son? What's clearly in focus for you, easy to spot, like those big letters at the optometrist's office? In knowing and relating to your son, what is almost second nature to you? And on the other hand, what is so small you can hardly see it? What is there about being a dad that's still out of focus for you? What stretches you right now? What is hard to see? Difficult to imagine? What's still *fuzzy*?

Many eye prescriptions change and get stronger over time. And I find myself once a year sitting in that chair, hearing my eye doctor say over and over again, "Is this one better or worse? Better or worse? Clear or blurry?" But he has to ask me those questions in order to make exact determinations about how to help me see clearly.

So with that in mind, here is a "dad eye exam" that will help diagnose your father-son vision.

Imagine you're walking down a beach just as the sun is setting over the water. You glance down to notice a corked bottle partially buried in the sand. Picking it up, you brush it off to get a closer look, when suddenly the cork pops off and smoke begins pouring out of it. And then, *Poof!* a genie appears (hey, you know you've wished this would happen). And suppose this genie turns out to be the Dad Genie. Lucky for you, you're a dad! So this genie offers you *four wishes* concerning you and your boy. Three wishes is too boring and predictable. Besides, we're dads and we're special, so we get one more wish. So you've got four things to wish for your son and your relationship with him.

What would those four be? And keep in mind, you get whatever you wish for, no matter what it is. You can't change your mind afterward, and you can't turn your fourth wish into four more wishes. Whatever you tell the genie will ultimately become reality. Your wish is his command. So, dad, what are those four wishes?

Take a few minutes right now and write them down. Use the margin or a blank piece of paper. Maybe you'll come up with eight wishes, in which case you'll need to narrow them down. If so, think of those individual wishes like college basketball teams, allowing them to compete with one another until you reach your "Final Four." This is all a part of your vision exam, forcing you to make determinations to help define and refine your dad vision.

Okay. Assuming you've done that, now look again at those four things. How do they break down? Which of your wishes have to do specifically with *him*? Which focus on you? Which deal primarily with the relationship between the two of you? Do any deal with his present or future *behavior*? Or touch on the issue of *character*? Or financial security? What about his or your relationship with God? Or a future wife? Do any have to do with healing from past issues or experiences?

Looking at those wishes, you now see a bit more clearly what your vision is for your son. So, how do you feel about that? Are there any you would consider changing before telling the genie your final four wishes? Do any of these differ from the four you'd wish for another son, if you have others? That list represents your heart for your boy. It's a written expression of what lives in your soul for him. Your goal. Your dream. Your *vision* for him.

Most dads have dreams for their sons. And if you're reading this book, you almost certainly do. So ask yourself if you still have the joy, the dreams, and the commitment you had the day you first laid eyes on your newborn. Have those dreams grown? Are they being fulfilled or are they dying?

Now, after committing those four wishes to memory, take the list and put it in an envelope along with a current picture of your son. Seal it and put it somewhere safe. In three years, you need to open it and give yourself another eye exam to see if your vision is still clear or if you need to adjust your prescription.

The Game Clock

Yes, it's sometimes easier to dream when our sons are young—and when *we're* young! It's easier to dream when our boys are infants because the whole "dad-thing" is new and exciting to us. In many ways, boys are easier to parent when they're small. I mean, the issues are so much simpler then—changing diapers, feeding them, giving them a toy to play with, putting in a kids' video, smiling at them, and murmuring authentic baby gibberish (which we men have a natural talent for). And boys are also easier to persuade and impress when they're little kids. You can tell your five-year-old fictional stories of how you wrestled bears in the great Northwest and shut the mouths of lions with your bare hands while hunting in the Serengeti. How you single-handedly led your high-school team to victory in the final seconds of the state championship game or hit that game-winning homer in the bottom of the ninth inning. And junior will sit and stare at you with wide-eyed wonder, thinking, *Wow. My dad. He's the greatest!*

But then the years quickly pass and it's not so easy to impress him with your world-famous exploits. You only get a short season, and then you're no longer reading bedtime stories to him while he falls asleep in your lap. Before you know it, he's too big for your lap.

Your exploits become less impressive, and the story at bedtime is often replaced by a primeval grunt and a shut bedroom door. And you find yourself wondering, *Where did* that *come from?* (Remember, you grunted too when you were his age.)

All three of our boys played T-ball when they were young. One of them started his baseball career in a "micro-league," which was played on a scaled-down Astroturf field about the size of an average living room. But it was hard to think of it as real baseball because everybody got to bat every inning, nobody was allowed to strike out, and nobody kept score so there wouldn't be a "loser." Sorry, but that's not baseball to me. That sounds like something straight out of the *Idiot's Guide to Politically Correct Athletics.*

When we stepped up to the next level things got even worse. They allowed—no, make that *required* and *recruited*—*girls* to be on the boys' baseball team. I'm not a chauvinist, but c'mon. There should be times and places where a guy can hang with guys and girls can be with girls. And for me, the boys' baseball team was one of those places. Funny, but guys aren't allowed to play on the girls' softball teams. Hmm. Even more frustrating for me was that, at this young age, boys and girls are pretty much equal in their physical development. Some of the girls were just as good as the guys in hitting, running, and fielding. I guess it all boils down to winning games. Even at that level. Sad.

But, have you noticed, though, the amount of parent support at those T-ball games compared to their attendance at the more advanced leagues? It doesn't matter what the sport—baseball, soccer, football, basketball. For the little guys, the stands are packed shoulder-to-shoulder with moms and dads, standing, screaming their heads off, cheering on their sons and yelling at the umpires. And the concession booth is raking in the cash—selling hot dogs, snow cones, sodas, and snacks to little siblings and adults alike.

But as time goes on, the space between parents in the stands becomes wider and wider. The collective roar from the crowd is replaced by the scattered lackluster clapping of a few weary-eyed moms and dads. The blame for this absent-parent trend could be placed, of course, on poor scheduling of games or some other reason. But the cold, hard fact is that by the time our sons are fifteen and still playing baseball, many dads are simply burned out on athletics. Truth be told, sometimes the boys are too, but they just don't know how to express it. Everyone is tired of three games a week and being forced to sell candy bars for the team and the league. Add to this that these dads are getting older now and working harder than ever before, and the net result is a sparse crowd in the stands.

Now take this attendance scenario and transfer it to your life as a father. The truth is that most dads begin their parenting careers enthusiastically, clapping, cheering, supportive, energetic. But sadly, few stay the course and finish strong at the finish line. That's because being a dad is a long-distance run, and none of us get any training beforehand.

Can you imagine waking up this Saturday morning and being driven downtown and deposited at the start of the local marathon? Having never run or trained for such a race, can you imagine how unprepared you'd be? Can you imagine what your body might feel like after one mile? Three miles? Ten miles? Would you even make it that far? Would you be able to finish a race like that?

That's exactly what it's like at the birth of your son. Upon drawing his first breath, your son's arrival into this world takes you from wherever you are in life and drops you at the starting line of the dad marathon. You're already in the race—unprepared, out of shape, and unaware of the topography or map of the course. And unlike a twenty-six-mile, one-day jog, this journey lasts a minimum of eighteen years!

Feel tired yet?

Eighteen years sounds like a long time, doesn't it? But even so, it can pass by in the blink of an eye. Before you realize it, your son is out of diapers and into video games. You wake up one morning and his sweet, innocent voice has changed. Then you come home from work one day and he's driving. And suddenly he's gone.

Many years ago I was attempting to install a deadbolt lock on the front door of our first home, a 1920s, 1,200-square-foot bungalow built in the historic Heights neighborhood of Little Rock. And because of its age, it was in need of constant repair. But this particular day I wasn't having much luck, as this was my first time to install such a lock. Frustrated, I paused and looked down to see a four-year-old boy staring up at me, complete with teddy bear under one arm and his favorite blanky under the other.

"What doin', Daddy?" he inquired innocently.

"Nothing, son. Daddy's working. Go find Mom," I abruptly replied.

Unphased, Clayton repeated his question. "What doin', Daddy?"

"Daddy's working, Clayton. I can't talk or play with you right now, okay? I'll play with you later."

He wandered back to his bedroom and resumed his playtime. Beverly, who'd been eavesdropping on this little father-son interchange, stepped into the living room and calmly offered an editorial comment.

"You know," she said, "he won't always ask 'What doin', Daddy?' Before long, he won't be interested in your household repairs. Besides, all he really wants is just to be with you."

Ouch!

Okay, enough said. With her mini-sermon still ringing in my conscience, I found Clayton and invited him into the living room. Once there, I placed him in my lap and explained to him the monumental importance of installing a deadbolt lock on a front door. I told him how putting in this lock would mean the door would shut properly, keeping out the wind, the rain, the cold, and most of all—the bad guys.

I concluded my speech by asking, "Clayton, would you like to help Daddy fix the front door?"

His big blue eyes brightened. "Yes sir, Daddy!"

"Okay. Hand me that hammer and let's get started!"

What had begun as an interruption ended with an opportunity to bond with my son. And I'm so glad it did.

That was fifteen years ago. And it went by so fast.

My friend, time does not stand still for your son . . . ever. He will not stay a little boy. He can't. He's changing and growing even while you're reading this book. And he won't wait for you. He has to keep growing and changing, and he'll do it with or without you around. So, dads, we must realize a sense of urgency in the time we have with our sons. This perspective encourages us to take advantage of the opportunities life hands us every day. We can't afford to be like I was that day—so focused on the task at hand that we miss the chance to spend time with our sons.

Hey . . . do me a favor. Pause for a second and hold up your ten fingers. Are you able to count on them the number of years you have left with your son before he leaves home? Can you count those remaining years on one hand? A few fingers? A couple of years ago, I opened the flyleaf of my Bible and wrote down the names of my three sons. Beside their names, I put numbers representing how many years I had left with them. It looked like this:

Clayton: 5 4 3 2 1
Stuart: 6 5 4 3 2 1
Davis: 8 7 6 5 4 3 2 1

Each year I've scratched out another number, counting down like a game clock the time I have left with my boys. At this moment, I am down to zero, one, and four, respectively. Single digits. And for my oldest son, it's *months*, not years left. By the time I finish writing this book, I will have said goodbye to him, but more about that in a later chapter. Honestly, I can't believe how quickly time went by. Like a lightning flash, five years turned into a few months. Six counted down to one, and eight years became four.

This fall my son's football team had a historic season, going undefeated in the regular season and in the playoffs on their way to the state championship. Having been unfairly placed in a conference with schools three times bigger than theirs, this tiny Christian school kept soundly beating their much larger opponents. Then came the game we all dreaded—a matchup against the defending state champions. The opposing team poured onto the field that fall Friday night, their nearly one-hundred-man squad filling their side of the field from one end zone to the other. Compared to our forty or so guys, it looked like men playing boys. We were outnumbered and outmatched. They were bigger and better. Or so everyone thought.

But what Clayton's team lacked in size, they made up for in raw talent and heart. Thanks to outstanding performances by some key players, our team at the end of the fourth quarter had amassed an amazing lead—44 to 7 over the defending state titleholders. And in our league, whenever one team gets a thirty-five-point margin over the other team, the officials invoke what is known as the "mercy rule," meaning the clock keeps ticking no matter what. They do this so the game can hurry up and end, saving the losing team from further embarrassment. Our opponent, out of time-outs, could do nothing but watch the clock wind down to a brutal and humiliating loss.

Similarly, there is no stopping the clock for dads and their sons. It ticks and ticks and ticks. No TV time-outs. No pause for injuries. No resetting the clock. Just the consistent movement of time. And we are powerless to stop it. And *that's* why we cannot afford to get behind in this game.

Your boy is growing. He's becoming. And your primary role in life is to prepare him for the day when he won't need you anymore. Don't be fooled by the illusion of *quality time*. That idea was invented to relieve guilt for dads too busy or too unwilling to spend time with their sons. In reality, quality time only exists within the greater context of *quantity* time. Therefore the clock is not your friend. That's why you must take advantage of the time you've been given. The game is progressing. The clock is ticking. Can you feel the urgency? Seize the moment, Dad!

A Built-in GPS

Many of today's traditional, "prescription" parenting methods usually involve simplistic, nice-sounding formulas. They look good on paper, but are another story in real life. Mere recipes for raising kids can't produce the end result we're looking for. Oh those methods may corral some unhealthy behavior through putting the "fear of God" into our sons. But your goals for your boy involve something deeper and better than his simply becoming a morally upright, churchgoing, law-abiding citizen.

GPS

Once, while attending a conference of youth leaders, my wife and I were standing in line for lunch when we engaged a fellow conferee in conversation.

"So you're a youth minister, huh?" the man asked.

"Yes, sir," I responded. "Have been for many years."

"Well, the way I see it," he said, volunteering some unsolicited advice for ministry, "if you can just get a teenager through high school—straight, sober, and still a virgin—then you breathe a sigh of relief and pat yourself on the back for a job well done."

I wanted to hit him in the face.

It's not that we don't want our boys to embrace moral purity—this book devotes two whole chapters to that. It's just that having morality as the ultimate goal misses the point altogether. It's a swing and a miss. In kid-raising recipes, that's a good way to turn your son into a little Pharisee—a boy under the illusion that his *goodness* is really the goal. We don't, of course, call those kinds of folks Pharisees today—but you know the type. They disguise themselves as faithful churchgoers, wearing a thinly veiled attitude of *I'm just a little bit better than you.* And they're glad they're not like those heathens out there in the world. But we've got enough of that kind already. Let's aim for something more. Something better for our boys.

A dad's vision must go beyond just helping his boy achieve morality. We want our sons to grow into the total-man package. Good behavior doesn't count unless the heart is engaged. Anybody can curb behavior with enough threats and penalties. But only the kind of dad who is *connected* to his son can reach his heart. That kind of dad is the wise dad.

Wisdom.

Now there's a word for you. It's the kind of word you hear more at church than at work. But it really applies everywhere. Wisdom is the ability to navigate through life by choosing the best path for the highest good. Wisdom is the one quality we desperately need as dads and yet it seems so scarce today. Maybe Solomon understood this and that's why he described wisdom as being better than silver or gold (see Prov. 3:14; 8:19).

As I mentioned before, this journey of fatherhood involves many unexpected twists and turns. Though "true north" stays the same, the way to your destination will require several course adjustments. That's because the road map changes and things aren't where your map said they would be. How frustrating! There's construction on life's highways and you're forced to reroute or divert, and that slows you down. Sometimes as a father you get stuck in a parental traffic jam, or have a flat tire. You may even have "relationship wrecks" along the way. Or you may find yourself "rubbernecking" as you slowly pass by a three-car pileup involving another dad and his son, whispering a silent prayer of gratitude that it wasn't you and yours. Then again, maybe you've already had some near misses or some fender benders of your own.

So because you never know what lies around the next bend, you have to be prepared to flex. This means that to some degree, you will have to grow along with your son. You won't be able to lead your son, for instance, in something you yourself have yet to experience. You can't give away what you don't possess. Therefore, you can't afford to get stuck in your own personal development as a man. You have to nurture your own heart and connect with God and with significant relationships that stimulate your inner growth.

To become the dad your son needs, you'll have to take your parenting off cruise control and keep your eyes on the road, ready to make those unexpected course adjustments. When my youngest son, Davis, was a little boy, he was fascinated with trains. No, make that obsessed with them. Train toys. Train rugs. Train bedspreads. Train videos. We rode train-like rides at amusement parks. We took rides on real trains together. Do you have any idea how hard it is to find a real steam engine train these days? I even taught myself to imitate the sound of a train whistle (which makes me glad he didn't develop an obsession for dolphins!).

But as Davis got older, he eventually grew out of his fascination with trains. Currently, it's guitar, football, and soccer. Which is cool for me, 'cause I play guitar. So it was fun for me to teach him how to play guitar, and I now serve as his in-residence instructor. Football has been fun for me as well because I love to throw and he loves to catch. We also share a love for movies and we have a twisted sense of humor, as do my other two boys. Like father, like son, right?

But the soccer thing . . . well that's been a bit more of a stretch for me. I didn't grow up playing soccer. No one in my neighborhood did. It just wasn't an American sport yet when I was young. Besides, I couldn't understand any sport that didn't allow you to use your hands. Consequently, I'm not as familiar or as passionate about soccer as I am other sports.

Nevertheless, Davis and I spent hours into the night putting together this ginormous soccer goal in the back yard. And I drive him to the soccer field occasionally so he can practice his moves and develop his skills. We help him purchase special soccer cleats, which are so expensive I'm convinced they have gold imbedded in them! And of course we attend soccer games.

My point? I've had to flex and become whatever he's needed me to be for him. Being flexible is part of reading the map. *Becoming* is listening to that inner GPS voice navigating the road and keeping the bond strong between us. It's also a part of realizing that, though I'll benefit greatly from this relationship, it's really not about me. It's not about what I get from him, as if he somehow existed solely for my pleasure and benefit. Rather, it's about what I can give *to* him. At the heart of being a dad is a deep commitment to absolute selflessness.

Think about that for a minute.

To be honest, there are things I wouldn't have ordinarily or naturally done unless I'd had sons. I wouldn't normally rise at four in the morning to sit silent and motionless in a deer stand for hours. But I'll do it for my son, even though I actually enjoy more active hunting. There are tons of things my sons have taught me to enjoy—things I might not have otherwise discovered had God not given me boys. Together, my sons and I share a love for action movies, sports, Apple computers, playing guitar, Monty Python, estate sales, sushi, bonfires, writing, and a host of other interests. But more than all these things, we share a love for each other. We share a bond as strong as steel, thanks in part to that flexible inner GPS.

Yes, there are things that all dads instinctively feel—things that magnetically pull us in the right direction in the father-son relationship. But for me, my relationship with my sons has been, more than anything, an overflow of my relationship with God. The stronger my heavenly Father-son relationship has been, the stronger has been my relationship with my boys. Having a strong relationship with God is not, though, a formula or some kind of guarantee. But think about it. A man who is genuinely in touch with his Creator-Savior will likely also show humility, faith, transparency, growth, vision, sensitivity, understanding, forgiveness, tenderness, and love.

How can someone who is experiencing those traits *not* pass them on—even if only subconsciously—in his relationship with his son? How you relate to your son is inseparably linked to what kind of a person you are. If you are growing in love, you can demonstrate how your son can do the same. If you are a caring dad, you naturally model that to your boy. If you are doing your best with challenges at work or home, you can show him how to navigate those waters. If you are processing life honestly, then you can portray that authenticity to him. Whatever flows *into* us from God can potentially flow *through* us and into our sons.

Think now about those four wishes you made earlier. Are any of those things currently true of you? Are you intentionally pursuing the things you desire one day to describe your son? Are you growing in your relationship with your Father? Are you experiencing a strong bond with Him? Do you have quantity time with Him? And I'm not referring to the infamous Christian "quiet time" once a day, but rather living a lifestyle in rhythm with Him. Are you learning to think your thoughts to Him, sharing all of life's experiences with your Savior? The joys, surprises, emotions, adventures, disappointments, hopes, and struggles that life unexpectedly throws your way? Are you walking in desperate dependence on Him through this massive challenge called *fatherhood*?

Do you breathe God like air?

Is He more to you than religious information? More than a duty to fulfill? More than an accessory or an add-on to your life? More than Someone to pay homage to once a week at "God's House"? Are you consumed by Him? Candidly, your greatest asset as a dad is the authentic connection you have with your Creator. Please reread that last sentence slowly. Out of this one connection flows everything you and I really need in fatherhood—wisdom, strength, patience, character, endurance, growth, manliness, sensitivity, grace, mercy, and love. These attributes have to flow in before they can flow out. God is your rock and anchor.

Cultivating a walk through life with the God who made you is the secret to fatherhood. And here's something else. That same God is wildly in love with you. Despite your faults and failures, in spite of your pride, stubbornness, even your weakness about lust. God sees through that veneer that many men call manhood. We men often cover our hearts with a shield, allowing virtually no one inside, not even God. But to be the dads we desire to be, you and I have to allow Him to crack that hard shell and to remake us from the inside out. To make our hearts His comfort zone.

Forget the past. Forget who you were. Who you are becoming is now your focus. No matter what your past, you can still hear your Father say, "I love you, son. And I am so proud of you for wanting to be the dad your son deserves."

God is your true north. Your vision. Your compass in the storm. Your vantage point.

Near the conclusion of that family trip to New York, we decided to visit the Empire State Building. But to our disappointment, the line to the elevators was hours long, so we concluded it wasn't meant to be and started to leave the lobby of the world-famous skyscraper. But while checking our map and looking like typical bumpkin tourists from Arkansas, an old gentleman in a blue sport coat approached us.

"Have you all been to the top?" he asked kindly.

Startled, we all looked at each other.

"No sir," I said. "I'm afraid the line is a bit too long for us today, and we're on a pretty tight schedule."

"You look like a good family. Are you? Are these good boys?"

Puzzled by his question, we all nevertheless nodded affirmatively. Then he leaned in closer.

"Shh. Don't say a word. Just follow me and stay close."

And with that he walked to a roped-off area, lifted the rope and motioned for us to come on through, right up to the elevator. Soon the doors opened and we were herded inside—just the old man, the operator, and the Kinleys. After an express ride to the top, the doors opened again, and there we were—on top of the Empire State Building! We stepped off the elevator and turned to thank the kind old gentleman, but he simply waved with a smile as the doors shut. And he was gone.

We have no idea who this man was or why he did that for us. But there we were, eighty-six floors above Manhattan. The vista from that high up was jaw dropping. From that vantage point, we could see for miles. From that perspective everything about the confusing maze of the city suddenly made sense to us. What was unclear from street level came into focus at the top.

As dads, we need that kind of perspective on raising boys. That's because the view on the ground can be frustrating, making it easy to lose our way on the road to our destination. That's why we need a GPS. A satellite view to help us see what we can't see by ourselves. So, may I ask you . . .

Have you been to the top?

CHAPTER 3

Tattoo Studio

Strength and power. Two things that capture a man's attention. As men, we have a natural attraction to things that burn, explode, and spin . . . things that *do* stuff. It's an obsession that actually begins when we're boys. I mean, it's a natural curiosity to wonder what happens if you put a firecracker inside a soda can. We love to blow things up, and we live for that split second when things go "Boom!" Have you ever seen on TV when an old building or stadium is being imploded? Wouldn't you love to do that?

Fire is another one of our favorites—campfires, backyard grills, fire pits, blowtorches, and Bunsen burners. We enjoy the feeling of grasping a Roman candle and having miniature meteors shooting from our hands like we're some mythical Greek god. Oh, the power of combustion! The rush that comes from holding a bottle rocket down to the last millisecond before launching it into the atmosphere! There's nothing like it. In fact, we guys like fire so much that sometimes we light matches just for the fun of it . . . just to see them flame up. We like to watch stuff burn, and it fascinates us to see what fire does to different things—from marshmallows to Styrofoam cups to small insects.

Men and boys gain great satisfaction from sitting and poking a fire. We can sit for hours, staring at a campfire, hypnotized by the glow of its embers, the dancing colors of the flame, and the heat that scorches our jeans. And when we can't actually make fire, our surrogate flame is a huge Maglite or even one of those 15 million candlepower floodlights mounted on the pickup truck. Lighting up the darkness of the woods or the back yard is such a cool feeling.

We also love taking things apart to see how they work or just to see what's inside of them. We enjoy the feeling of power that comes from operating electronic devices, like the TV remote for example. I think every newborn boy should be given a toy remote—you know, so he can get the feel of it and practice until his time comes. Maybe we should start burying men with their remotes in their hands, as this is usually one of their most valuable possessions this side of eternity.

We like controlling things and being in charge. Recently a friend of mine who is in the Air Force let me fly in a 200 million dollar simulator. Oh man, it was so realistic! Climbing into the cockpit, I "flew" over places in the world where . . . well, let's just say it's *classified*. The high-res detail on the screen was better than any video game you can imagine. But just knowing I was in control of the plane—even if it was in simulation. Wow!

Most men like to operate large machinery. And few things rival the feeling we get when handling a power tool. It doesn't matter what kind of tool. Air compressor, nail gun, circular saw, chain saw, lawn edger . . . you know the drill (pun intended). We like the feel of power flowing from our hands . . . or foot, as in pressing the pedal to the metal on a car just to see how fast it'll go.

We like building things, then standing back and admiring our work. We construct backyard decks and love bragging about how you could drive a truck over it.

And we love guns. Perhaps nothing taps into a man's passion for power more than a firearm. I live in Arkansas, where we love basically two things—the Razorbacks and hunting. You see a lot of camouflage here. It's everywhere—camouflage on trucks, four-wheelers, and of course clothing, all the way down to our boxers and boots. We call it "camo" for short, like we invented it or something. In the fall, thousands of camo-clad men disappear into Arkansas Heaven, a.k.a. the "deer woods."

It's like a pseudo rapture. Work desks are suddenly empty. Lawnmowers left running in the yard. Tractors abandoned in the fields. Even TV remotes lay motionless beside the couch. All because the hunter has gone into "the woods." Once there, he settles into his perch, patiently waiting for hours in the deer stand . . . in stone-cold silence. Finally, the moment arrives. The game is in your sights. You zero in just before you gently squeeze the trigger. Then there's the sharp report of the weapon fired. The flash of the barrel. The millisecond of impact. The animal hits the ground. And you begin to celebrate the takedown.

Afterward you drag the deer carcass to the four-wheeler, carry it back to the deer camp, hang it up, and skin it. For me, that's about where my feminine side kicks in. I prefer going from kill to eat, skipping straight over that "skin and process" part. But it's a timeless ritual, really. A rite of passage for thousands of men and their sons. We don't do many debutant balls here, but we do get our boys' pictures in the sports section, holding the antlers of their first kills. And men return to the lodge and tell tall and detailed narratives of how it all went down, kinda like golfers in the men's grill after a round on the links.

Only with more camo.

Granted, not all men hunt or target practice with pistols and rifles, but for the majority who do, it's an awesome feeling. But hunting's just a part of experiencing a piece of something bigger encoded deep down inside us. It's that God-given desire to exert energy. To exert power . . . or at least to see it demonstrated. Not the kind of power used to dictate a country or to abuse employees. But the kind that gives us vicarious satisfaction—like when a defensive back blindsides and levels a receiver. Or when a slugger connects at the plate, sending a baseball rocketing five hundred feet over the center field wall.

It's the reason we buy oversized golf clubs, so we can "feel the power" of a three-hundred-plus-yard drive. Something that compels us to impact. To make a difference. To feel the power and contentment through what our hands have done.

But there's another power that men possess and enjoy. Something that transcends race, religion, social standing, and sports. Hunters and golfers alike possess this power. So do businessmen, plumbers, electricians, and that guy who installs your car stereo. But harnessing this power doesn't involve a trip to the hardware store or loading a weapon.

This power is more potent than a stick of dynamite and more permanent than a construction project. Using it properly requires more skill than golf, more ingenuity than rebuilding an engine, more patience than hunting, and more planning than remodeling your kitchen. But it brings more satisfaction than anything you've ever done at work—bigger than a huge commission, and more profitable than securing a massive deal or seeing fourth-quarter profits rise to record levels. This power carries with it more exhilaration than being with a beautiful woman. More joy than ten Super Bowl wins and being voted into the Hall of Fame or winning an Olympic medal.

I'm talking about the raw power you have within you to shape and influence your son. To mold him. To imprint his mind. To stamp his heart. To tattoo his soul. It's not a special power reserved for "great" dads, and it's not an ability some dads have and others don't. It's not reserved for the rich or the smart, and it's not a gift given only to those who seek it. It's not something that can be abdicated to a coach, teacher, mentor, or pastor—though these are an important part of the picture. No, this power is something unique that every dad possesses, regardless of background or faith, finances, personality, or marital status. Put simply, if you're a dad, you already have this power. And to quote a famous superhero movie, "With great power comes great responsibility."

Dynamite Dad?

You may be wondering, *How did I get this power? I mean, I didn't ask for it. And what does it really mean? How do I use it?*

You received this power when you had sex and God made a life through that unifying act. You gave the sperm. God did the rest. As in a presidential inauguration, you were "sworn in" with this power the day you became a daddy. With the creation of that new life, you were immediately endowed with great influence. No, you didn't become leader of the free world or CEO of a large corporation. You became something a whole lot more important. The titles "Mr. President," "Your Excellency," and "Your Honor" don't hold a candle to "Dad."

44

Over the years I've known hundreds of dads like you and me, thrust into fatherhood unprepared, but with all the enthusiasm of a kamikaze pilot. We begin our dad careers determined and focused—our game faces set toward a big win in the world of fatherhood. Some of the dads I've known have grasped the power confidently in their hands, ready to use it in the best way possible and for the highest good of their sons. I've watched these dads assume their role with the deepest conviction and commitment. These are the guys who decide early on that being a dad will be their number-one pursuit—ahead of job, career, and even their personal hobbies and interests.

That was true of my own dad. Born and raised during the Great Depression, he worked his way through high school at a local ice cream parlor until the day he looked old enough to join the Navy during World War II. After the war, he settled down to a simple life in a small South Carolina town. And as each of his three boys came along, he quietly did his duty as a dad. Verbal communication was not his forte, but Dad did his talking every day of his life—in going to the job, displaying a fierce work ethic, and coming home for dinner every night at six. In fact, Mom and Dad both worked full-time to make ends meet and make sure we always had what we needed.

We never had an abundance of "stuff" growing up, no second home or fancy vacations. But, honestly, we never really cared for all that. Most of our summer weekends and vacations were spent camping at nearby Lake Hartwell. Despite not having a lot of things, we had what every boy ultimately dreams of—a secure and loving home.

My dad had been an outstanding baseball player at the Navy's Staff College during the war. And I'll never forget, as a small boy, seeing him round third base in a church softball game and slide into home. When the Carolina dust settled, home plate had been completely uprooted from the ground, the umpire yelled "Safe!" and Dad had a broken leg.

J. B. Kinley made sure he was there at virtually every one of his sons' ball games, cheering us on from the stands. My father did the best he could to the best of his knowledge. He used the power well, and all these years later, I'm a better man because he did.

Obviously not all dads know what to do with this power.

Consider Eli. A priest who lived in Israel many years ago, he was also dad to two sons—Hophni and Phinehas. But though he was a minister to God's people, Eli's own family was a wreck. His two sons are described by the Bible as being "worthless men; they did not know the LORD" (1 Sam. 2:12 NASB). Nice legacy, huh? But that's only part of the story. These two scoundrels were stealing what was offered in worship to God, plus they were having sex with the girls who served in the tent of meeting. Their actions couldn't have been worse. Scripture goes on to paint a picture of their father, too, that is less than favorable. And the emerging portrait is of a dad who apparently was weak-willed, consumed with his job, negligent of his family, and afraid of his sons.

Eli had the power. But he didn't use it wisely.

Through apparent neglect, laziness, or simple preoccupation, his dad power was misused, producing very unhealthy results. Perhaps he developed a hidden fear of his sons when they reached puberty. After all, lots of folks do. I meet people all the time who confess to me, "I don't know how you work with teenagers. With their clothing, piercings, language, music, and overall attitude, they intimidate me. They're obnoxious!"

I can understand why someone might say something like that. Those kinds of statements, however, usually come from people who haven't taken the time to know teens. If they had, they'd discover that teenagers are just people—not aliens, mutants, or social deviants. They're just kids on the road to adulthood, navigating their way through the confusing maze of adolescence. But to the average adult, they can be extremely intimidating.

So it's possible that Eli, like a lot of dads today, found himself faced with a fifteen-year-old boy who was rapidly showing signs of adulthood, including a serious case of rebellion. It happens to a lot of dads. Your son starts to grow big physically, plus all of a sudden he's the world's reigning expert on just about everything. With the sprouting of a few chin hairs, he suddenly needs no more advice from Dad. He's got life all figured out. Mom and Dad are now outdated, like yesterday's news or last year's technology. And what's worse, he even challenges your authority at times.

In short, he thinks *he* has the power now.

So it becomes your job, dad, to help him work toward manhood without crushing his God-designed desire for independence. But at the same time, you have to help him grasp the concept that you're still in charge.

Eli failed to do that.

As a result, his sons, even in adulthood, disrespected their father. And it brought him great shame.

The power of a dad is real. The power is undeniable. It's like you're the star player on the team, and everyone knows it. You can choose to sit on the bench or take the field. Either way, the outcome of the game will be greatly affected by your choice. The power is yours. The power teaches. The power molds. It's unleashed every time your son looks to you. That's just the way God made boys. This power is on your son like hot or cold, and you're the thermostat. It's inherently affecting him whether you're present or absent. He can't help it. He has to succumb to it. Like air, he has to breathe it in. And your inherent father power is matched only by your son's equally passionate desire for you. Sons want to feel that dad power flowing through their lives.

Getting It Right

Writing a book like this makes me a bit hesitant to share some of my rare "greatest hits" as a dad, lest I give the impression that I think I'm the world's greatest dad. I know better. So do my boys. My episodes of stupidity are legend, and I have more than my fair share of dumb-dad moments. Like the times I've allowed my pride to get the best of me, and I become a rock of self-righteousness, refusing to lose an argument with one of my sons. I've been stubborn, even when I know I'm losing the verbal sparring match and my logic sucks. But I keep pressing on, looking like an idiot in the process. Like running out of bullets and desperately throwing my gun at the enemy. Yeah, like that's what a man really is—someone who can verbally or mentally outmaneuver a sixteen-year-old.

Right.

So I have plenty of cracks in my male armor to be sure. But a few specific instances in my being a dad stick out in my mind as highlights. Times when the power was flowing in the right direction. Usually it's the everyday things, the nuts and bolts of the father-son relationship, that have been so memorable and had such impact.

Like the time we were driving home from church and a voice from the back seat broke the silence. "Dad, you know what?"

"What's that, buddy?" I responded, glancing into the rearview mirror.

"You're just like God," the prepubescent voice said.

I was so shocked by that statement I almost ran off the road. After regaining my composure, I attempted to respond in a reasonable tone of voice.

"What do you mean by that, son?" I said, having no earthly idea what was about to come out of his mouth.

"Well, just the way that you've never broken a promise to us, and how you always keep your word. That's what God does."

You'd think that after hearing my son say something like that, I'd be washed away in a tidal wave of pride. Actually the opposite happened. What welled up inside me were tears, so much so that I could hardly see the road. It was one of *those* moments. A time when I sensed the power had flowed from me and hit him square in the heart, leaving a permanent tattoo—the good kind.

I was so humbled as I drove the rest of the way home, reflecting on all the times when I was sure I'd let my three boys down. Times when I'd failed them by not living up to my word. Times when I'd said the right thing but didn't mean it.

As we turned into the driveway, I managed to mumble, "Thanks, son." I watched all three boys run to the house, and it occurred to me that, whether I realized it or not, I'd been broadcasting an invisible message about God simply by the way I daily interacted with my boys. And my son had picked up on the frequency. Something was coming through loud and clear. And for that I gave thanks to my Father.

Another time was when my oldest son turned eighteen and, after steaks on the grill, we were celebrating in the back yard with his first cigar (though I'm not advocating here the use of tobacco). I'd made a visit to the local pipe and tobacco shop earlier in the day, inquiring about what kind of cigar I might buy for a young man on his eighteenth birthday.

"You want him to throw up or enjoy it?" the man at the shop asked, an unlit stogie protruding from his mouth.

"I'd like him to enjoy it, actually," I said, smiling.

And so, later that evening, as Clayton and I were about halfway through smoking our Arturo Fuente cigars, he paused, blew a thick cloud of smoke into the evening air and said, "Dad, how do you do it?"

"How do I do what?" I replied, typically oblivious as I created my first-ever smoke ring.

Clayton continued. "I mean, the way you've always known how to guide me through life. In every situation you've always known the wise thing to say to me. You've always given me just the right balance of loving discipline and direction. You've always known exactly what to do, and in the right way."

What do you say to a statement like that, spoken by a boy crossing the threshold into manhood? I thank God I had enough sense not to go into a lecture or to hijack the conversation and "sermonize" on him. I also didn't want to play the worm and deny his tribute to me, robbing him of the moment's joy. So I paused and the words simply came. "Clayton, I guess it's because I've tried to follow God and because I just love you more than life itself."

"Hmm," he said, nodding, as if he was filing that thought in his mental archives to use later on in his own life.

And we smoked our cigars.

All of us, to some degree, blow it in the dad department from time to time. All of us. Me and you. At times we feel like we've failed. Like it's over. We've made mistakes. We've had setbacks, maybe even gotten off to a slow start. But just remember, we can start slow and still finish strong. Better *that* than to be like most fathers, who start strong, only to peter out at the end. They start with a bang and end with a whimper. But that's not us. And that's not you.

Dad, this power is yours. It belongs to you. And that power is unleashed, not with a ball of fire or the thrust of a rocket, but rather a little bit at a time. Controlled. Throttled up and down as needed. It's released daily in the trenches of life. At breakfast. Dinner. In the back yard while playing catch. Before bedtime. On the way to school. On weekends or after a big game. It's more about being than teaching.

Some books about fatherhood will give you ideas on how to create memorable moments with your son. That's great, especially when you need some creative inspiration. But even better than *creating* the moments is *catching* them. The slogan for one insurance commercial is, "Life comes at you fast." Bingo. That's because you can't always create the wind, but you can catch it. Those opportunities are all around you. Look for those moments to influence your son through everyday life. Not to control him or dominate him. But simply to allow who you are as a father to naturally flow to him. Savor those moments. Enjoy them. Inhale this father-son aroma as deeply as you can. Don't allow the hustle of the daily grind to rob you of life's greatest experiences.

As you continue growing as a father, you'll start sensing the right way to use the power. You'll know what to do when the time comes. Your influence in your son's life penetrates below the surface, like a tattoo.

And generations later, it will still be there.

CHAPTER 4

No "Mini-Me's"

Surrounded by nearly-naked men, I was noticeably uncomfortable being the only guy in the room with clothes on. But before you get nervous and jump to conclusions, allow me to back up and give you a view through the wide-angle lens.

I'd traveled to Indianapolis to do research on my book *Through the Eyes of a Champion: The Brandon Burlsworth Story.* Brandon was an All-American guard for the Arkansas Razorbacks, and he'd been drafted in the third round by the Colts. They were excited to have him on board after he'd made an impressive showing at the NFL Scouting Combine.

Just days following his appearance at the Colts training camp, though, Brandon was tragically killed in an auto accident. I was now tackling the huge task of writing his inspiring biography. As part of that research, I was spending a few days conducting interviews with players and coaches at the Colts' Indianapolis facility. That's why I was in a locker room with half-naked men.

You can now breathe a sigh of relief.

Glancing at the physical specimens strutting around that room, I was overcome with a huge feeling of inadequacy. All around me were muscle-bound guys who were ripped from head to toe. I'm talking gladiators with chiseled frames. Well-defined pecs, bulging biceps, and rippling, six-pack abs, which were as common as hand towels in that room. The only thing out of place was me!

When I'd concluded my interviews, I stood up, turned around, and realized I'd been sitting in front of Peyton Manning's locker the whole time. I paused and let my eyes caress that sacred space, thinking, *This is pretty cool.* I mean, we're talking about a Super Bowl MVP, All-Pro quarterback, and certain future Hall of Famer. A super-jock if there ever was one, a franchise player, and a cash cow of endorsement revenue. Standing there, I could almost smell the money . . . if it weren't, that is, for the stronger odor of sweat mixed with after-shower cologne.

Come to think of it, maybe Peyton Manning's not such a wonder of nature. Maybe he's not quite what he appears to be. Peyton Manning comes from a legacy of athletes. And not just athletes, but great athletes. Specifically, great quarterbacks. His dad, Archie Manning, was an All-American college football player and an NFL MVP. Peyton's younger brother, Eli, would eventually become a Super Bowl MVP. Cooper, the eldest of the Manning boys and a high-school standout in his own right, had his football career cut short when a congenital spinal condition was discovered. But still, he had the "juice." Three boys, all of them outstanding football players.

Just like dad.

Hmm.

Now it's entirely possible that Archie Manning "just happened" to sire three sons who amazingly inherited the physical and mental ability to play football better than anyone else in the whole world. Their predisposition toward near supernatural gridiron talent may have come naturally without any persuasion and pressure from a father who also excelled in the sport. In which case Archie Manning certainly won the lottery and gives a whole new meaning to the phrase "dominant gene." What dad wouldn't be proud to have three boys so naturally gifted?

Or there's also the possibility that the three Manning boys never really had a choice in the matter. It's possible that their football futures were predetermined by their father long before their tiny hands threw their first spirals. Maybe it was decided early on that they would all play. And that they would be good. Very good. No matter what it took. Since football was of such high value to Dad, perhaps he determined that the sport would also become a top priority to his sons.

Maybe making football their focus was how the Manning boys received positive affirmation and attention from their dad.

The Manning boys could simply be "three in a million." Or ten million. Crazy anomalies of nature. Like lightning striking three times in the same place. Since I don't know the inner dynamics and history of the Manning family, I'll assume the best and guess that Archie had some part in his boys' success.

Currency Exchange

I have many faults. I don't multitask very well. I sometimes procrastinate. I've been known to leave hair in the sink. I criticize people who drive like idiots. But of my many faults, *not paying attention* doesn't rank among them. Observing people and life is a hobby of mine. And as I've observed and worked closely with dads over the past two decades, I've noticed a reoccurring theme. I watch fathers consciously and unconsciously force their sons into a mold that bears an uncanny resemblance to dear old dad himself.

Take "Phil," for example. He loves golf. It's his favorite hobby. No . . . make that his passion. *Obsession* is an even better word. Sounds more manly than *hobby*. Phil plays golf once or twice a week, sometimes more. When traveling for business, he always takes his clubs and wears a sleeveless windbreaker monogrammed with the name of the latest golf course he's played. It's a badge of honor for Phil to let everyone know what links he's conquered. At Phil's office, golf magazines are spread on the table in his waiting room. Golf-related paintings adorn the walls, with a special rendering of the twelfth hole at Augusta hanging over his desk.

Phil plays with a regular foursome each Saturday—and Thursdays, too, when he can sneak away from work early. After each round, the four of them gather at the men's grill and rehash each hole, shot by shot. They laugh as they replay the shanks and slices of the day, the monster drives, the putts that lipped out. And the four of them settle up on dollar bets, handing the lunch ticket to the man with the worst score.

So that you don't think I'm ganging up on golfers, you should know that I play occasionally myself. And when I connect in the tee-ing area, you need satellite tracking to keep up with my drive. Usually I land somewhere in the fairway, too. Unfortunately, it's not always the fairway of the hole I'm playing. The problem is not that I don't like golf. The problem is that golf doesn't like me!

Phil's problem is not his golf game. He's no duffer. In fact, his nickname is "Scratch." And there's nothing wrong with Phil having a passion for a sport like golf. As men, the older we get, the fewer num-ber of sports our bodies allow us to play. Phil's real dilemma is that his son, Jake, hasn't shown much affection for the game, preferring instead to ride motorcycles. And to make matters worse, the sons of Phil's friends all seem to have a natural affinity for swinging a club. That makes Phil feel awkward when the others go for those father-son golf outings.

Early on in his life, Jake figured out, of course, that when he played golf, he earned the enthusiastic approval of Dad and got to spend some real time with him. Otherwise, the unspoken message was that he didn't quite measure up as a son. But as he's gotten older, Jake's love and skill for dirt biking has far outweighed the pursuit of other sports. It's even trumped his desire for that affirmation he used to get from his dad. Today, Jake gets a much bigger buzz from jumping moguls than from chipping out of sand traps.

And there's an awkward distance between father and son.

As dads, we may subtly place unfair pressure on our sons to ex-cel in sports. Applying pressure may not be a conscious thing, mind you. But we do it nonetheless. Football. Baseball. Basketball. Soccer. Golf and others. And why do we do this? Sometimes we do it because that's where we got our own adolescent buzz back in the day. We want our boys to feel the sweat, the thrill of team sports, the exuberance of winning. We just want them to know how much fun it can be to play sports. Nothing wrong with that, right?

Other times, though, we're subconsciously hoping they'll turn out to be the athlete we never were, achieving the glory and adulation we never had. And we end up living our lives through our boys. But doing that is just as sad as a thirty-something mom who still dresses and acts like a high-school cheerleader because her daughter finally made the squad. You just wanna walk up to her and say, "Give it up, grow up, and move on with life."

How many boys, though, have endured a childhood of being force-fed an activity that was, in reality, the currency of exchange for gaining the attention, affection, and approval of their dad? You know what I'm talking about. For some dads that currency may not be athletics, but rather things like popularity, academics, music, business, student government, community service, or getting a part-time job at fifteen . . . just like Dad did.

I wish I could tell you that I was once a great athlete. I mean, I did have a few bright athletic moments as a boy. As mentioned previously, my dad was a very good baseball player, and all three of his sons were all-stars in the sport. I did win the state championship in Punt, Pass, and Kick. And I had a forty-two-inch vertical jump in high school, a five-foot-eleven boy who could dunk. But with no ball-handling skills, all I have to show for my exploits now are some tarnished trophies, faded newspaper clippings, and a few cool stories. And who cares, right?

The real athlete in the family was Mom. While in high school, Beverly set a state record in the high jump, winning the Arkansas State Championship in the event three years in a row. And her record stood for over ten years. She was even offered a full track scholarship to the University of Arkansas, a program that has won forty national titles in track and field and cross-country. So somewhere in the back of our minds, Bev and I were convinced we'd produce at least one great leaper, but so far that hasn't panned out.

It turns out that each of our three boys are separate and unique creations. And although my sons and I share many traits, they are not mini versions of me, or "mini-me's."

Your son is not you, either, Dad. God made one of you. Period. And He made a separate creation when He hardwired your son. The world doesn't need another Phil. And trying to turn Jake into Phil would be like David wearing Saul's armor. It just doesn't fit. But the world *does* need Jake to be the best Jake he can be. If that includes golf, then so be it. But it doesn't have to. Trying to turn a boy into a "mini-me" is a tragic mistake, and in the process Dad can do great damage to his relationship with his son.

There's a big difference between encouraging our sons and pressuring them. And maintaining a balance is like walking a tightrope. On the one hand, your son may have actually inherited the DNA and desire to follow in your footsteps with regards to athletics, music, business, academics, or even ministry. He may be as naturally gifted and determined as you are, and if so, your job is to help him uncover and develop his area(s) of passion. You do this by exposing him to a wide variety of activities and experiences early on in his life, gently guiding him along the way.

Our son Clayton, for example, enjoyed many years of playing baseball, but by age thirteen it was becoming increasingly clear that he was not cut out for the diamond. The desire and ability simply wasn't there anymore. We did the same with Stuart regarding sports and even music. We bought him a guitar, thinking he may have inherited my natural ability to play by ear. It wasn't there. But instead of being disappointed, we celebrated. That just meant we were one step closer to discovering where his real passion and talents lay. On the other hand, our youngest, Davis, picked up the guitar and started strumming like he'd been playing it for years.

Clayton eventually discovered football, largely because of his hormones kicking in at age thirteen, and he desperately needed an outlet. "I don't wanna touch the ball, Dad," Clayton announced. "I just wanna hit somebody!"

"Well, son," I responded, "football is one of the few sports you can play where you can hit somebody as hard as you can, and hundreds of people will stand on their feet and applaud you for it."

Sports and other activities can serve a purpose even if they last only a short while. The real question you have to ask is what's best for him *right now*? His hobbies and activities will likely change several times. He won't always be a football player, a Boy Scout, or a budding rock star. But he can gain some valuable lessons and experience as he participates in a variety of activities and interests. Keep in mind, too, that he'll probably change his major a few times in college . . . just like Dad!

Let me tell you, though, what's really important: that our boys don't find their ultimate identity in what they *do*. Even if proficiency in athletics or academics earns them a scholarship, those particular abilities will, in reality, be short-lived. Experts predict that the jobs our sons will eventually hold haven't even been invented yet.

All this to say that discovering your son's current interests and abilities doesn't mean his path is set for life. It just means you have a better idea on how to navigate life with him for the time being.

Apart from his interests, activities, and hobbies, your son's natural personality and temperament is also a clue as to how you can guide and interact with him. Is he a natural extrovert? Reserved and contemplative? Overly curious or compliant? Conscientious or creative? A dreamer or the possessor of a meticulous mind?

If we believe that God made our sons, then it makes perfect sense to discover that divine design and get on board with it. Solomon, one of the wisest men who ever lived, once wrote, "Train a child in the way he should go, and when he is old he will not turn from it" (Prov. 22:6).

We typically think of "training" our kids like a teacher or personal trainer would—with lessons and lectures. This is the thinking of traditional "Christian parenting" as well. But this isn't exactly the imagery Solomon had in mind. In other Hebrew literature, the phrase "train up" is used to describe the rubbing of juice or crushed grapes on a baby's gums and palate in order to produce a sucking response. The idea is that the child would develop a natural affinity for nourishment. The correlation is that parenting is an opportunity to create an environment in which our sons will have a healthy thirst for God and for life. This book is about ways we can create that environment.

But the second part of Solomon's saying goes beyond mere "training," to training specifically "in the way *he* should go" (emphasis added). Train him up in *his* way, not your way, the church's way, another parent's way, or the way his brother should go.

But *his* way.

One of the struggles we face in the Christian subculture is the pressure for our kids to dress, talk, or act a certain way. There's often a preconceived image of what a "Christian child" or "godly teenager" looks like—his hairstyle, musical tastes, reading material. Ask anyone, and that person will be more than happy to give you an opinion on how to raise your boy. This kind of "checklist Christianity" has no place in your boy's journey into authentic manhood. God didn't call you to take a public opinion poll. Who your son becomes is not about other people, anyway. If we're too concerned with what other parents or the church thinks, then we'll never be able to lead our sons to be the men God wants them to be. His opinion and design, after all, trumps all others. Other male influences will be important in your son's life, but ultimately your son is a stewardship from God.

Solomon suggests that you zero in on your boy alone. The phrase, "the way he should go," refers to the bend of a bow, as in a bow and arrow—something Solomon would have been very familiar with in his day. This bend refers to a boy's natural gifts, talents, abilities, and personality. Your job is to help your son use these God-given traits to his advantage, and to recognize that a boy is most happy when he's being himself. Learning his bent, though, takes time, observation, study, personal interaction, some experimentation, and most of all . . . relationship.

My three boys are all very different from each other. Clayton, our first, put his mom through about twenty-four hours of labor before being born. We thought he'd *never* get here. Finally, my wife yelled at the doctor, "Just pull this thing out of me!" So the doc grabbed these giant salad tongs and pulled him out. Late for his own birth, all through high school he was the last one ready for school each morning.

Stuart, on the other hand, quietly and almost stealthily slipped into the world early on a Sunday morning without fanfare or crowds. Today he's an astute observer, doesn't crave attention, and when he speaks, people listen carefully or laugh at what emerges from that brilliant mind.

Davis, like a typical third-born, came bursting out of the womb, kicking and screaming, waking half the maternity ward and causing the other half to go into labor. We took a snapshot of him when the doctor held him up, as he literally took his first breath of air. He has a mouth the size of Dallas. He hasn't stopped talking since.

Three boys. Each one as different as daylight is to darkness. One night some time ago at dinner, we were laughing about something when Davis slapped the table, causing his glass of milk to go flying. Clayton, as the eldest, felt it was his duty to scold his younger sibling, instructing his little brother concerning exactly what he had done wrong to cause this dinnertime calamity. Stuart immediately jumped up to get a dishtowel, and Davis . . . well Davis just laughed even harder. At times their differences have, of course, sparked conflict. Like the time two of them were arguing over something in the kitchen when a full-blown fight erupted. I sat at the kitchen counter and watched, thinking, *Wow. This is better than Pay-Per-View.*

We're thankful, however, that the physical altercations have been few and far between. The three boys remain close to each other, despite their God-designed differences.

Brothers.

Every boy is different. And that includes yours. He's a unique creation. A one-of-a-kind thumbprint made by your heavenly Father. As such, part of your dad-duty is discovering that design and working in partnership with God so your son can become the man he's meant to be. Athlete. Artist. Activist. Engineer. Writer. Dreamer. Visionary. Soldier. Mathematician. Designer. Musician. It doesn't matter. What does matter is that we don't try to create sons after our own image.

If God made your boy into a six-foot-seven drink of water, it's fairly obvious he's not destined to be a jockey. But other things are not so clearly discernable. That's why you have to be patient, yet deliberate and intentional in understanding your son. The better you understand him, the better you can help him reach his potential and achieve his destiny.

The "Big Borrow"

Once Jesus told a story about a wealthy man who went on a journey. Before leaving for his trip, he called three of his servants together and asked them to take care of his finances while he was away. To each of these servants, he entrusted different amounts of treasure to invest in his absence. Upon his return, the owner was interested in what the servants had done with these treasures:

The man who had received the five talents brought the other five. "Master," he said, "you entrusted me with five talents. See, I have gained five more."

His master replied, "Well done, good and faithful servant! You have been faithful with a few things; I will put you in charge of many things. Come and share your master's happiness!"

The man with the two talents also came. "Master," he said, "you entrusted me with two talents; see, I have gained two more."

His master replied, "Well done, good and faithful servant! You have been faithful with a few things; I will put you in charge of many things. Come and share your master's happiness!"

Then the man who had received the one talent came. "Master," he said, "I knew that you are a hard man, harvesting where you have not sown and gathering where you have not scattered seed. So I was afraid and went out and hid your talent in the ground. See, here is what belongs to you."

His master replied, "You wicked, lazy servant! So you knew that I harvest where I have not sown and gather where I have not scattered seed? Well then, you should have put my money on deposit with the bankers, so that when I returned I would have received it back with interest.

"Take the talent from him and give it to the one who has the ten talents. For everyone who has will be given more,

and he will have an abundance. Whoever does not have, even
what he has will be taken from him." (Matt. 25:16–29)

Notice how each of the servants treated the treasure entrusted to
him by his master. Two of the men treated the treasure in such a way
that doubled its value. But the third servant chose instead to dig a hole
and hide what his master had given him, thus netting a great big zero
for the estate. This did not make the owner happy. To the first two,
the master gave nothing but praise. But to the third servant, the master gave nothing.

Playing it safe isn't always the best way to go, especially when it
comes to the treasure God entrusts to his servants. Apparently He
likes it when His servants exercise faith mixed with a little risk. And
while Jesus wasn't speaking about the father-son relationship in this
story, there's still a great parallel here for us dads. While we're here
on earth, God loans us things—time, money, energy, talents . . . and
sons. These are all things that rightfully belong to Him. They're His,
not ours. But He lets us take care of them for a while, just like the
master in the parable and his treasures. It's a test, really. A stewardship
to see what we'll do with what He gives us.

Some men are hard workers while others struggle with apathy and
passiveness. Some are natural risk-takers while others prefer to stick
with the sure thing and follow a safe route in life. Some men like to
guard while others would rather gamble. Part of stewardship, then,
has to do with temperament and natural bent. The default mode. But
some of it also relates to a daily choice we make by faith. We choose
to trust in a God we cannot see but whom we embrace deep in our
hearts. If we think of our sons as treasures given to us by Him, our relationships with our sons take on a whole new perspective.

After all, children are a gift from the Lord (see Ps. 127:3). But
they're not the kind of gifts we get to keep forever. A later chapter
talks about a time when we have to let them go.

A key to understanding fatherhood is coming to terms with this issue of stewardship. It's a very serious and sobering realization. God lets
us borrow our children from Him for a few years. In reality, our kids

don't actually belong to us. I mean, we call them our own, but they're not actually ours. They belong to God and are merely on loan for a while. And while we have them, we have a fantastic opportunity to help prepare them for life. It's the biggest and best stewardship of all.

Admittedly, it's a hard concept for us to swallow, and perhaps even more so for the fathers of sons. That's because there's an element of ego involved, which is linked directly with our own sense of manhood. And nothing intimidates a man more than when he feels like his manhood is threatened. But as men, we have a choice to make. We can view our boys as objects to control, like a power tool, business deal, or a big game to win. Or we can put our selfish pride in storage and see our sons instead as treasures to be nurtured and developed.

One day we'll give an account to our Master of how we invested in the boy-treasure He loaned to us. Have you ever thought about that? Have you ever wondered what God will ask you about the stewardship of your son? Ever thought about Him reviewing what you did with the gift He gave you? I ask, not to put you under a cloud of unnecessary fear or guilt, but rather to sober us all up. After all, there are times in life when every dad needs to man up. When we need to step up to the plate, even when we're afraid of striking out. Honestly, having a son is a massive responsibility, and one that can almost overwhelm us at times. But it's a part of authentic manhood to take responsibility for our lives and our actions. To take seriously the mission God assigns to us.

God gave you a son. That gift is a stewardship. A treasure for you to manage, invest in, nurture, and develop. One day when you release him and present him back to God, you want to be able to say you did your best through God's strength.

So because each boy stands as an individual before Him, the greatest thing a father can do is guide his son in the way destined and designed for *him*. To take him to a place where he can stand on his own in a big world. But that can happen only in the context of a very special kind of relationship.

The father-son kind.

CHAPTER 5

Trust Fund

Grandparents can be really cool people. I was fortunate to have two sets of pretty great ones, especially my grandmothers. Part of what most impressed this boy about them was their cooking. Their prowess in the kitchen was legendary, evidenced by the dozens of grandchildren and their families gathering regularly for meals at their homes. My granny Kinley made the best—and sweetest—iced tea you could possibly imagine—true Southern style. It was so dark you could hardly see through the glass! And her homemade biscuits were *huge*, about the size of hamburger buns!

On the other side of the family, my grandmother Poore's specialty was fresh vegetables—corn, beans, tomatoes, and okra—prepared well in advance and in big portions, and just the way all vegetables were meant to be cooked . . . *fried*. But another one of granny Poore's specialties was dessert. Her coconut cake was so moist the juice would ooze out of it as your fork cut through a piece. Another delectable dish of hers was banana pudding. Sweet. Creamy. Packed with fresh bananas and vanilla wafers, topped with a thick layer of meringue. I can't tell you the number of Sunday afternoons I spent at her house, devouring huge bowls of that Deep South delicacy. Fortunately for me, her talent in the kitchen was a gift she passed on to my mom.

But that same grandmother passed on more than just recipes. When I was still a little boy, Granny Poore opened up a savings account for me with a whopping initial deposit of twenty-five dollars. I was eight years old at the time, and that sure sounded like a lot of money to me. I was told that this money would become mine upon my graduation from high school.

So I spent the next ten years dreaming, wondering how much would be in that account when I finally withdrew it. I couldn't wait for my graduation day and to get my hands on the loot that had been multiplying there all those years. When the day finally came, I made the trip to the bank, walked up to the front counter, and requested my money, expecting a large dividend. But after a few minutes, and to my dismay, I was handed a check written in the amount of about thirty-five dollars! Not exactly the lump sum I'd envisioned.

In my warped understanding of banking, I'd dreamed of taking that money and going on a shopping spree. But what I failed to understand was that initial twenty-five dollars would not and could not grow unless someone kept making additional deposits into the account over the next ten years.

Standing in the bank lobby, the depressing reality hit me right in the wallet. There was no large withdrawal waiting for me. No big check. No spending spree. No celebrations. That's because, generally speaking, the rule of banking is that a few small deposits equal small returns. But many deposits over time equal big returns. That was a hard lesson to learn for this Southern boy. As I recall, I went home and drowned my sorrows in a big bowl of banana pudding.

Reality Checks

When it comes to a dad's relationship with his son, there's a striking similarity between building a savings account and the way a father builds trust with his boy. As I write these words from the second floor of a local coffee shop, I can see a popular investment firm located directly across the street. On their window are posted current CD rates and investment option returns. The idea is that the firm takes your money and, at least theoretically, makes more money for you—and consequently for them as well. The same principle applies to fathering, and the result is a good return on your parental investment, and one that's protected even if the stock market crashes.

The way this investment is protected is through establishing trust and earning respect. These two components are part of the glue that bond a father and son together. The bank is your relationship with your boy. Withdrawals are what you make when you need something from the relationship—like when you discipline your son, when you ask him to trust even though what you're saying doesn't make sense, when you have to say no to something he really wants, when you're giving him advice. The older he gets, the bigger the withdrawals become. Denying your four-year-old a lollipop, for example, is nothing compared to telling your seventeen-year-old he's grounded from using the car for two weeks. During times like these you'll wish you'd made lots of deposits over the years.

But withdrawals are also made, just like regular savings accounts, when you want to take money out to do something fun, like taking him on a trip, running an errand to the hardware store, or helping him work through a family argument or tragedy. The enjoyment of your relationship with your son is directly determined by your investment into this account.

You may be wondering, *What's the big deal here? If I'm the father, then I'm in charge. What I say becomes law, right? If I'm the authority in his life, then why should I care if he likes it or not? I'm not running a popularity contest here, am I?*

It's true that you are his authority, but just because you're the dad doesn't always make you right. Your position of authority should never be used as an excuse simply to bring the hammer down regardless of how it impacts your son. Sure, life is filled with instances when you have to be the "heavy" in spite of your son's inability to understand your reasoning—as in, *Because I'm your father* or *Because I said so.*

Relating to your son only from a position of authority, though, will eventually backfire on you . . . big time. And here's why. Merely contributing sperm doesn't automatically deposit a single dollar in your dad-son bank account. What it does is simply give you access to the savings account number and the privilege of making deposits and withdrawals. It's up to you to build up the account. Being in the position of dad gives you the opportunity to create a *relationship* with your son. If you operate only out of authority, you'll create only distance and rebellion in your son. Guaranteed.

And the bank account will be bone dry.

So how can you be a rich man in this area? How can you build a hefty relationship account from which to draw and to enjoy?

Body Armor

Earlier we discussed this law of time in parenting—*quantity* time trumps *quality* time. But in reality, the quantity begins very early on in your son's life. Trust, like most savings accounts, is built little by little. It begins the first time you hold your newborn son. It's developed when you toss your boy up in the air and catch him. He subconsciously learns that Dad will be there to cradle him and break his fall every time.

Once when our family went swimming at a local pool, I decided to persuade my son Stuart to jump off the low dive into the water. As I waited in the deep end of the pool, Stuart strolled out onto the edge of the board and confidently announced, "Well, I know one thing. My daddy won't let me drown." And with that, he jumped in with full assurance that I would be there to catch him. Though he was only five at the time, he was banking on past times when I'd proven my dependability to him.

As men, every time we follow through on our word, we strengthen the bond in our relationships with our sons. It's that bond we want to develop with our sons, a bond not unlike the unique fabric that makes up what is popularly known as Kevlar, or body armor. Worn by soldiers and law enforcement officers, this vest protects its wearers from bullets and even shrapnel from grenades. But the secret to the vest's enduring strength is found in the multilayered, tightly woven fibers, five times stronger than steel. Imagine that! It covers the vital organs of the body, preventing a fatal wound.

The father-son bond is like that Kevlar vest—strong, tightly woven, and able to protect you against the missiles of the enemy that will surely come. It's designed to keep the relationship from suffering a fatal wound. And each time we build the trust factor with our sons, we weave that fabric a little thicker and a little tighter. Conversely, each broken trust leads to a tear in that fabric and makes your son vulnerable to harm.

Right now, I'm in a season of life when I'm enjoying multiple benefits from years of building equity in my trust account with my sons. Don't think I'm claiming to be without conflict or challenges in my relationships with my boys. I'm light-years from perfection and in no way better than other dads. I tell you the truth—it is still hard work to be a dad. It requires sacrifice every day.

But as someone has wisely said, "The trouble with life is that it's so . . . *daily!*" And yet, isn't that the best way to live? Not that we don't make plans for the future, but that we simply realize that all we ever really have is right now. None of us are promised a tomorrow (see Prov. 27:1; James 4:14). So we have to make the most of what we have now. That means being intentional about every day of our lives, especially when it comes to our boys. We have to remember that he's a boy only once. He gets only one childhood. There are no repeats, reruns, or turning back the clock. If you miss his first few steps, then you just miss out. There are no second chances with firsts like that. In order to build a big bank account with your son, you have to be there. This is nonnegotiable.

I realize that your job may require you to travel or be away from home. You're not alone in that respect. That's the case with many dads. And it makes us feel good that we're providing for our families when we're away at work. But in the midst of those professional demands, we have to make sure that our sons are not neglected. No advancement up the corporate ladder or promotion in the company can ever replace what we miss by not being with our sons. And if we choose fatherhood over career, we'll have to deal with the feeling that inevitably comes if our peers fly by us on the road to riches. As they zoom past us on their way to "success," we may feel like stranded motorists on the side of the road. That's a risk you take when you put your son first.

Building a relationship with our sons isn't rocket science. It all boils down to a simple matter of priorities. Not the priorities we write down on a piece of paper, but the ones we live out every day of our lives. The ones our calendars reflect. The ones our evenings portray. Put plainly, we *get* what we *give*. The more we invest, the greater our return. It's as basic as that, and an unbreakable law of relationship economics. Don't be fooled into thinking you'll be the first one to suspend that law. Being a dad to a boy is a huge honor, and one that should be taken with a certain degree of "fear and trembling." We cannot parent by proxy or from a distance. Fatherhood is a one-on-one sport. We simply have to be there for them. It's one of life's greatest privileges that also carries huge responsibilities.

Perhaps nobody abuses this privilege more than ministers. There's a huge temptation in my line of work to put "God's business" ahead of family. And doing just that is a rampant epidemic in my profession. This was painfully brought home to me—hard—one night following the birth of our first son. As an enthusiastic young youth pastor, I understood the value of spending time with teenagers on their own turf, doing the things they enjoy. It's a primary way youth pastors relate to youth. A missionary mind-set.

So this particular night I was over at a kid's house where a few of us were engaged in a marathon Monopoly game. We had a blast, and the game didn't end until about 3 AM. As I recall, I ended up with Baltic Avenue.

After racing home, I made like a Navy Seal on a Special Ops Mission. I snuck in the front door of my house and tiptoed into my bedroom under cover of darkness. But just as I was about to crawl into bed, the light came on. My wife, who just weeks earlier had given birth, sat up in bed and gave me a look that told me I was in trouble . . . the deep kind.

She proceeded to remind me that my days of hanging out until 3 AM were officially over now that I had a newborn son. She continued her lecture by informing me I had entered a new stage of life, one with family responsibilities. A new mission now superseded even my calling to ministry. In short, there would be no more marathon Monopoly games until the early morning hours. I stood there, speechless, feeling like I'd just been sent to jail without passing Go or collecting two hundred dollars.

So I quietly listened to what the "Holy Spirit in a nightgown" was saying to me.

She was right, you know. I now had a new, and much more important priority. Something more immediate than reaching teenagers. Something more important than "church work" or ministry. And so, convicted in my heart and convinced of my role, the following week I told my youth group how much I loved them, and reaffirmed my commitment to spend time with them. But in the same breath, I also announced to them that my family was now number one, and that my commitment to my son would now take priority over my youth ministry.

Little did I know at the time that my dedication to being a better dad would also make me a much more effective youth minister, as I began understanding teenagers from a parent's perspective. It also demonstrated to my students the value of family.

As our family has grown, we've kept that same value with us as priority. And over time, it has been severely tested. Once, when working on staff at a megachurch, my boss wanted me to be out an additional night of the week to visit new church prospects. The point of my job was, after all, to get new members—a.k.a. "tithers"—into the church. But because of my prior commitment to family, I flatly refused, citing my boys as my priority, not to mention that I was already out two other nights a week with ministry. When I was told that I might have to look for another job if I didn't comply, I responded by stating, "That's fine. There are a hundred guys I know who would love to be the youth pastor at this big church. But I'm the only man on the planet my three boys call 'Dad.' And I'm determined that I won't hear them say one day, 'Dad, where were you when we were growing up?'"

A few months later I walked away from the corporate megachurch Christian world for good.

Did that decision cost me? I suppose it depends on what you really consider valuable in life. To this day, Beverly and I have an understanding that I will not be gone away from home on speaking engagements for too many days out of the month. She has access to my schedule and veto power over my calendar. I have learned that many times my wife can see—or even sense—when work is becoming too much of a beast in our schedule. As for me, I decided that career simply wasn't worth it. You'll have to weigh the pros and cons and make your own decision. But be careful. You may conclude that your job isn't worth what you're missing at home. You may find that you've been padding one bank account while bankrupting another.

Have I missed out on some opportunities for ministry by staying home? Maybe even some financial gain or book sales on the road? Sure. But the payoff has come in all the "firsts" I've been there to witness. All the Friday night football games I've seen. All the family nights I've enjoyed. All the deposits I've made. In over two decades of working with dads, I have yet to hear a single man say to me, "Jeff, I wish I hadn't spent so much time with my family."

Dad, the number-one rule of fatherhood is *Be there*.

Integrity

Granted, our boys need male role models. Examples. But a role model is not an NBA superstar who suits up and shoots a basketball better than anyone else. Rather, it's someone who personifies integrity in his personal life, over time. Contrary to what popular culture might want us to believe, there are no "snapshot mentors." No quick fixes in fatherhood. No drive-through dads. Nothing of lasting value usually happens overnight. Integrity is a function of character, and is developed over a lifetime.

If we're honest, however, we'd have to admit most of us men have blown it in one way or another, haven't we? Maybe you've gotten off to a slow start as a dad, or had some serious setbacks. Maybe you've done damage to your relationship with your son. You may be a single dad or have suffered through a bitter divorce. Perhaps you feel like you've failed as a father. In that case, I have some good news. You're surrounded in life—at work, at the club, in the neighborhood, and at church—by men just like you who have failed their families in some way. We've all missed the mark.

So the question isn't whether you've failed. The real key to restoring your role as Dad is admitting those failures and then moving on. Maybe you need to ask forgiveness from your wife or children. If so, then do it. Admitting failure is tough, especially when circumstances, people, and even your own heart reminds you of those sins and shortcomings from time to time. But failure never has to be final. The race isn't over yet. So get up. Brush yourself off. And give yourself lots of grace. You'll need it—because you'll fail again, soon.

If we allow failure to stop us, though, we've played right into the Enemy's hands. He loves nothing more than to paralyze us with past defeats, bludgeoning us into ineffectiveness. But remember that some of life's greatest heroes also experienced huge failure and disappointment. In the pages of your own Bible are men who blew it big time. Moses was a murderer. David was an adulterer. Jacob was a deceiver. Samson was filled with anger and lust. Peter was a wimp, who denied Jesus. But every one of those guys finished strong. Each of them refused to let their past weigh them down. Remember, you can't run a good race while looking backward. So don't focus on what's behind you, even if others may. Don't allow the sins and mistakes of the past to sabotage your resolve to make the best of fatherhood.

Integrity is not defined, then, by a lack of failure or by the presence of perfection. The real question is what about *now*? What about *today*? What are you currently doing that is causing you to be a man your son can admire? How are you pursuing a life worthy of imitation? Are you striving for personal excellence? Are you real with your son? Are you honest? Are you true? Do you ask forgiveness and mean it? Integrity involves authenticity. Does your son ever see you get emotional? Has he ever seen your eyes filled with tears over a scene in a movie? Have you ever gotten emotional about your relationship with him, or with Jesus?

Do you live out the sermons you preach to your family? Again, it's not about perfection, but rather about progress. Integrity refers to what you're made of. It's who you really are. And no matter how much you try to be something else, the real you always shows through. That's because who we are in real life is an overflow of who we are inside.

And the people closest to us usually know the real inside story. A man recently heard I was writing a new book and asked what it was about. I told him it was a dad-to-dad conversation about how men can have a kick-butt relationship with their sons. Without hesitation, he asked, "Do *you* have a kick-butt relationship with your sons?" To which I rapidly replied, "I sure do." But in retrospect, I shouldn't have answered that question. I should have said, "Why don't you walk across the room and ask my sons?" That way the man would get the straight truth. My sons know if I'm real or not, and they'll tell you. They know some of my faults and failures too. It's easy for me to talk—or write—about integrity, but for the real story, ask my three teenage boys.

That's because integrity is more than just a principle or an ideal. It stems from character. And character is like blood; when cut, we naturally bleed it. Like sweat, it seeps through our pores every day as we live our lives. That's one reason why our word is so important. As we discussed earlier, it's crucial that we make only those promises to our sons that we intend to keep, and that we keep all the promises we make. But beyond that, your son needs to know that his dad doesn't even need to make promises. His word is enough. A dad who can be relied on is a dad with integrity. He's a man who's making deposits into that father-son trust fund.

But it's not just your sure word that builds up that account. It's also important for your boy to see you model integrity in your decisions. For him to know that you do what's right, even when no one else is looking.

Integrity and trust are also deposited into our father-son accounts through *listening* to our sons. Every time you open your ears instead of your mouth, you communicate a value that says, "You're important to me, son . . . You *matter*." Admittedly, sometimes what our boys talk about may not affect national security or seem important to most adults. They may want to tell us about a new video game, a cartoon, a soccer goal, the latest NFL score, or a funny scene in a movie. Your boy may chatter on about stuff that has no apparent bearing or relevance to your life . . . or anyone's! But if it's important to him, it needs to be important to you.

If we expect our sons to listen to what we say, we have to cultivate a climate in which the words and thoughts our sons convey matter. Everyone in life has a God-given urge to matter, to count for something. And no relationship matters more to your son than the one he has with you. When you listen, it says to your son that you respect him as a person. And it's another deposit made into the account.

Culture Club

Another way to build integrity and credibility with your son is by taking time to get into his world and to understand it. By being aware of his culture and genuinely interested in it, you show him he's significant and thus close the generation gap. This isn't so much an issue when he's a toddler, but as he grows, so do the challenges. Granted, sometimes it's hard to relate to our kids because it's been so long since we were children. We forget what it's like. But try to remember what it was like when you were a kid, how every day was a new discovery. And how the culture around you shaped a large part of who you were.

In approaching the subject of culture, it's important for us to remember that not everything about it is bad. We need to be careful not to approach culture—media, movies, music, fashion—out of fear. Fear will only lead us to removing ourselves from culture or condemning it from a distance. Both are unwise and unbiblical approaches (see John 17:15). Too often Christians are perceived as ignorant, narrow, repressive fanatics whose only emotion is anger and who are sadly lacking in the reasoning department.

But that's not you. And I believe God is asking us to help change that perception in the world. Doing this requires us to be more than just morally upstanding rule-keepers. We must go deeper than that, more toward a life guided by love and wisdom. That involves recognizing that within every culture, there are healthy and unhealthy influences. There are also moral, immoral, and *amoral* values. The moral and immoral ones are pretty easy to spot. Those are the ones that are obvious—the blatantly righteous and unrighteous.

That other category, though, makes it tough, and requires us to engage our minds . . . and God's. In the *a*moral category are things that are neither inherently good nor bad. They just *are*. They are there in culture, and it's our choice to use, enjoy, embrace, change, challenge, or avoid them. But in order for us to make intelligent choices, we have to be able to *interpret* our culture. Again, the traditionally accepted model would be to label everything either *good* or *bad*, *godly* or *ungodly*. But a better way would be to use God's wisdom, rather than simply to float downstream without thinking.

To accurately interpret the culture in which your son finds himself, you first have to know it. That doesn't mean you're a world expert on every musical genre and every Hollywood release. And it won't require you to become a techno-savvy media guru. But it does mean you know enough to make intelligent, informed decisions without coming off sounding like a complete dork to your son.

This means you keep your eyes and ears open. It means you watch some movies and TV, read some magazines, and listen to some music. Most of the discussion for Christian parents in this area usually involves how to limit your kid's exposure to culture—and there certainly are some things to avoid. But again, that's a defense mentality motivated out of fear. And while you don't want to indiscriminately expose your son to things he shouldn't see, hear, or experience, at the same time, your job as a dad is to do more than simply *protect* him from harmful influences. You have to take the next step and *provide* him with a rich, healthy cultural experience that shows him how to enjoy his culture without being negatively influenced or swallowed up by it.

Protecting our sons is somewhat of a default mode. But our job as dads is to provide fun, enjoyable, and healthy experiences for our boys. Whether it's movies, music, concerts, football games, hunting, or video gaming, there are great experiences and adventures out there for your boy—and for you—to enjoy. And that's why you have to know your son and his world well enough to know what's best for him. Talk to other dads. Older dads. Wiser dads. Engage your son's friends in conversation. Take him places. Do things together in guy groups. Camping. Concerts. Movies. Cookouts. Whatever fits him.

You may not be the hippest dad on the block. Your hair may be thinning while your waistline is expanding. You may not be able to talk intelligently about every music group or the latest iPod update. That's okay. What's important is that your son senses deep inside how much you care for him. That he sees the direction you give him and the decisions you make concerning his life as coming from a man who really wants the best for him. In doing so, you're winning his heart a little bit every day.

And that's a trust fund money can't buy.

CHAPTER 6

Clubhouse

Roots. They're what give life to a tree. Spreading deep and wide beneath the ground, they provide stability against whatever might threaten the tree on the surface, and add to the tree's longevity. Several years ago, we had a massive oak tree in our back yard in Mobile, Alabama, its branches reaching out for about forty feet in every direction. It provided much-needed shade from the oppressive Alabama heat.

While we lived there, this massive oak stood strong through four hurricanes, surviving with hardly a scratch while surrounding trees tumbled to the ground. The old oak never budged. Instead, it seemed to invite climbers, swings, and zip lines, beckoning little boys to dangle from its branches like monkeys. We loved that tree. It was a tangible reminder of things that endure. And because it wasn't going anywhere, we decided it was the perfect base upon which to build a tree house for three active young boys.

So after some gentle prodding by my wife, I consented to spend a Saturday knocking out this project. Besides, every kid needs a tree house, right? And this one would be a piece of cake since I was no stranger to construction. By the time I was a teenager, my dad and older brother had taught me how to swing a hammer and work a power saw with ease. (Just don't ask me about the chainsaw incident—it's a painful memory that involves broken windows, damage to my house, and a bruised ego.) But because of the instilled carpentry skills, I was ready to build this backyard tree house in a day.

Something happened that Saturday morning, however, as Beverly and I talked over coffee. The project began to take on ambitious dimensions. What should have been a few planks and some plywood nailed to a tree, morphed into a deluxe treetop resort, complete with poured cement, support beams, custom-built windows, curtains, a pulley system for retrieving and lowering objects, and, of course, a tin roof. I'm not exactly sure how this happened, but after my wife got involved in the planning and design, a leisurely afternoon in the back yard turned into a two-week construction project.

Women.

But in the end, we had one heck of a tree house. And the boys helped out, retrieving tools, carrying lumber, and even pounding nails. It took time, patience, and hard work, but the result was the coolest backyard tree house in town. No, make that the coolest *club*house, on whose door we proudly hung a sign that read "No Girlz Allowed."

Built on a Rock

One of the smartest men who ever lived wrote, "By wisdom a house is built, and through understanding it is established; through knowledge its rooms are filled with rare and beautiful treasures" (Prov. 24:3–4).

I'm pretty sure Solomon wasn't talking about bricks, mortar, wood, and nails. He wasn't referring to studs and joists, rafters or roofing. He was talking about a home.

Your home, Dad.

Building a relationship with my boys, I've discovered, requires similar construction skills as building Solomon's house. The essentials for building a good home, though, can't be found on the shelves of the local hardware store. They come from somewhere else. Another source, one outside the physical realm. And unless you and I are plugged in to this power source, we're gonna have a real hard time putting this father-son project together. In looking again at Solomon's proverb, I notice three words to describe how a home is built: with *wisdom*, *understanding*, and *knowledge*.

The words' meanings overlap some, but they're also distinct from one another. We could define them this way:

- *Knowledge*: Gathering the facts—sort of like going to the hardware store for basics like wood, nails, and screws.
- *Understanding*: Knowing how to put those facts together in their right relationship—like having a good blueprint or plan. You have an idea of what you want the finished product to look like.
- *Wisdom*: This is seeing how the knowledge and understanding intersect with our lives and relationships—like when you strain to dig the fourth posthole or nail the hundredth nail. As you do this, you can take a few steps back and see progress—that you're actually building a house.

Wisdom is living accompanied with skill. It's using knowledge guided by understanding. Wisdom can turn a house into a home. It can turn a father into a dad.

And it's this dad-son relationship that we're after. But in building this thing, we want to make sure we're not just throwing materials together. We can't just "get 'er done" so we can move on to more important things that afternoon—like college football. We can't wish our boys' childhoods away or fast-forward to a better day. We have to realize that being a good dad is more than merely providing room and board for our sons, making sure they're in a good school, taking them to church and on an occasional fishing trip.

As another anonymous wise man once said, "Anything worth doing is worth doing well."

And nothing is worth more effort than your relationship with your son. You want that house—or rather that clubhouse—to be a deluxe model. How, though, do you want to furnish this clubhouse?

Knowing that wisdom is not provided by a technical blueprint, we have to go beyond just a set of rules to guide us. You need more than a generic plan designed by somebody who doesn't understand you or your son. That's where we need the guidance and the hands of a skilled Carpenter. The wisdom God wants to give you will involve basic relationship skills, intuition, instinct, and even mysticism.

The support structures for this kind of clubhouse are the essentials every dad and son need. They are not built with lumber, nails, and concrete, but rather constructed with something a whole lot stronger.

Confidence

I have a photographic memory. It's a gift really, the ability to instantly memorize a face or an image and subconsciously store in the databanks of my mind. I should have worked for the CIA. Years, even decades, can pass and I can still recall with crystalline clarity faces and features. Names, however, are another matter altogether.

But faces aren't the only things I remember with precision. I can also recall the words people have spoken to me over the years. If you're like most guys, you can remember those school-yard nicknames, playground jabs, and locker-room comments. And maybe it's not just the ones that were aimed at you, but also the barbs you may have poked at others. Kids can be cruel that way. I can still call to mind the things my grammar-school teachers said to me, some of them good and some not so good. When we were learning how to write cursive in the second grade, Mrs. Sullivan pointed out to the entire class what a beautiful *h* I had composed. Pride beamed from my freckled face that day. I think it's still my favorite letter to write. Thanks, Mrs. Sullivan.

I also remember my sixth-grade teacher criticizing me publicly because I was a "hippie." She was a preacher's wife, a mean-spirited woman who had ugly knees. I made a mental note that I didn't like preachers, their wives, or ugly knees.

But one comment stands out above the others for me. It happened during my ninth-grade year. As a fifteen-year-old, I was a member of a basketball team that featured some of the best players in the city. I'd been playing basketball for only about a year, so I spent all my time "riding the pine." No playing time for Kinley. I was nothing more than side-court decoration. Filler. Like one of those skinny spare tires you use only in case of emergency. And you don't want it on for long.

Following a rather embarrassing practice one day, during which I'd drawn the laughter of all my teammates after taking a shot and missing rim *and* backboard, I retreated downstairs to the old basement locker room to clean out my things and go home. Earlier in this book I mentioned the importance of a boy's having male mentors besides Dad. Coach McClinton is an example. Sensing my discouragement, he followed me down there.

You need to understand that in the Deep South where I grew up, there were some pretty well-defined racial boundaries. Whites and African-Americans were integrated into schools, but that didn't relieve much of the tension that existed between us. One place where most guys were color-blind, however, was on the basketball court. For some reason, athletics has a way of breaking down barriers to help guys see each other as fellow teammates instead of racial opponents.

Coach McClinton was black and did a good job making sure there were no racial divisions on his team. In addition to that, he was also a great coach and human being. His door was always open, and he loved to bring out the potential in teenage boys. And so late that afternoon, as I stood there alone in the basement, frustrated, defeated, and stuffing sweaty clothes into a gym bag, Coach walked into that smelly locker room.

"Kinley, I hear you're thinking 'bout quitting the team. That true?"

"Coach," I responded, "I'm no good at basketball. Everybody knows it. The guys just laugh at me."

"That's not true, Kinley," Coach said. "You have great natural ability. You just have to work on it, develop it, and practice hard in the off-season. And if you do, I guarantee you'll come back to this team next year and be one of our starters. I know you will. But you can't quit, Kinley. You can never, ever quit."

Those were just the words I needed to hear at that moment. Words of encouragement. Words of hope. Words that said he believed in me. Words from a man I greatly respected.

Coach McClinton's verbal encouragement stuck with me, sinking deep into my memory. I *believed* his words and what he said about me. He filled me with confidence. So I worked hard in the off-season just like he told me to. And the following year I returned to that team and earned a spot on the starting five, becoming an all-star in the city league.

Words are powerful, friend.

Whoever said, "Sticks and stones may break my bones, but words will never harm me" was an idiot. No wound is so deep as the wounds caused by a cruel or unkind word. The power of the spoken word can send rippling effects throughout generations. And nobody's words carry more weight in a young boy than those of his father. Preacher's sermons fade out of memory. Teacher's lessons are often forgotten after regurgitating them on a test. But the things said to you by your dad imprint themselves onto your root system.

A boy's self-esteem is as fragile and transparent as glass. Words are like bricks: they can be used to build something, or thrown at a young man's self-esteem, shattering it into a thousand shards. Some boys later spend their entire adult lives trying to overcome the damage done by angry or discouraging words spoken to them by their dads.

Control over the tongue is a skill possessed only by mature people. Your ability to restrain yourself in difficult moments is part of what makes you a man. And it's what makes the difference in your son's view of himself and his relationship with you. Most of us men struggle to express ourselves positively in words because it requires engaging ourselves emotionally. And men sometimes have trouble doing that. But it's something we have to overcome if we want to really bond with our sons.

Your words have great weight and lasting impact in your son's life. This means you praise your son for his accomplishments—at school, on the team, with the band, in scouts, in his talents and abilities. But go beyond his talents and successes; praise him for *who he is*—his *character* and how you see him developing into godliness and manhood. Tell him how cool he is. How witty, intelligent, funny, creative he is. Brag on your son. We've lost the art of "That's *my* boy!" Hey, it's okay to be proud of your son and to tell others about it. You don't do it to make *you* look good, but to show others how great *he* is. Tell your son that you brag on him, and as you do, tell him how proud you are of him and how honored you are to be his dad.

I once said to my son Davis, "If I had a hundred lifetimes to live, I'd want to be your dad in every one of them." Anticipating an emotional response to this father-son bonding moment, Davis looked up at me and said, "Dad, your breath smells really bad."

Okay, so maybe I didn't achieve the magic moment I was looking for, but the words stuck with him. He knows I'm pumped beyond description to be his daddy. He knows I'd rather be Dad to him than write ten best-selling books. And because of this, he's confident. Not cocky, but filled with encouragement in life.

That's what I'm talking about. Positive words. Uplifting words. Words that encourage and inspire. Words that *build*.

That's one reason why every day of your life, you need to tell your son, "I love you."

Discipline

Friendship with your son is important, but you're more than just a buddy to him. A boy needs the strong, guiding hand of a father who isn't afraid to discipline him. I'm not talking about punishment here, but loving discipline. And the difference between the two? The two words do, after all, seem pretty similar in meaning. Punishment is when a person suffers the penalty for a crime committed. The only concern is that the guilty gets what's coming to him. Punishment is the ticket you get for speeding. It's paying a fine or being sent to jail. It has no thought of restoration or rehabilitation. The dad who merely punishes his son enjoys seeing him get what he deserves.

A judge punishes, but a father disciplines. Punishment administers consequences. Discipline serves a greater purpose, a better purpose. Discipline sees beyond the moment. God disciplines us as children, as the writer of Hebrews reminds us:

> And you have forgotten that word of encouragement that addresses you as sons: "My son, do not make light of the Lord's discipline, and do not lose heart when he rebukes you, because the Lord disciplines those he loves, and he punishes everyone he accepts as a son." Endure hardship as discipline; God is treating you as sons. For what son is not disciplined

by his father? If you are not disciplined (and everyone under-goes discipline), then you are illegitimate children and not true sons. Moreover, we have all had human fathers who dis-ciplined us and we respected them for it. How much more should we submit to the Father of our spirits and live! Our fathers disciplined us for a little while as they thought best; *but God disciplines us for our good,* that we may share in his holiness. No discipline seems pleasant at the time, but pain-ful. Later on, however, it produces a harvest of righteousness and peace for those who have been trained by it. (Heb. 12:5–11, emphasis added)

It's clear from this paragraph that God is like a loving father who disciplines his son. And what more perfect example could we have than Him? Clearly we should seek to model ourselves after His ex-ample. But it's also clear that discipline isn't fun for the dad or his boy. But it's still necessary—and much easier to do if you establish who's in charge at an early age. Good discipline from a loving father accomplishes two things: it *protects* and *provides*. It protects your son from attitudes and behavior that would hurt him—physically, emo-tionally, mentally, and spiritually. But it also provides for him a bet-ter way to see life and to live it. Again, if you don't start early, you'll pay for it later.

It was evident to us early on that the boy named "Tim" was headed for trouble. As early as fifth grade, he was making choices that raised red flags in our minds. And because Tim was a school friend of our son, this caused us some concern. So we sat our son down and ex-plained to him how we weren't ready to offer him the freedom and choices other parents were allowing their sons at this time. We also explained how other parents didn't discipline their kids the same way we do. Having worked with teenage boys for many years, it was easy to see where Tim's path would eventually take him. I'm not a prophet. Again, I just pay attention.

Beverly later followed this up in a casual conversation with Tim's mom, in which she proclaimed their philosophy was "letting Tim make his own mistakes." And he certainly did. In the absence of consistent loving discipline, Tim got into trouble at school, trouble at home, trouble with his girlfriend, and eventually trouble with drugs. His dad's response was to lower the hammer on him. Punishment. But it was a classic case of too little too late. That's because we can't ignore disciplining our sons in their early years and call in an air strike of tough love later on. It won't work. In fact, it will likely backfire on you, driving your son further away. And why? You've probably guessed by now . . . no relationship.

Tim's dad did exactly what *his* dad had done to *him*—waited too late in the game to start scoring points. And, like his own dad, he tried to make a withdrawal in that relationship equity account, but sadly, the account had been closed long ago.

Discipline begins the first time your son reaches for the wall socket and you pull away his hand or pat his little bottom. It continues every time he defiantly refuses to obey or hammers his little brother over the head with a plastic ball bat. As soon as possible, your boy has to know what's acceptable behavior and what will get him into trouble. But even beyond that, he has to understand, as explained by you, *why* those actions and attitudes are so unhealthy, harmful, and wrong.

In all your discipline, your goal is to do more than just correct or curb behavior. That's the easy part. But if you have a relationship with your son, with God's help you can make more than just a change in his actions. Following an incident during which five-year-old Clayton had shoved his younger brother off the bed, I was about to discipline him when he burst into tears. Turning to me, he asked, "Daddy, why do I do these things? What's wrong with my heart? I want a new heart."

So instead of disciplining his bottom, I invited him up in my lap and took time to show him how Jesus could give him that new heart he wanted. And right there in our bedroom, Clayton asked God to change him from the inside out. Jesus took his old heart of selfishness and gave him a heart of service and love. That happened, not because I was a minister, but rather because of a relationship I'd been cultivating with him for those five years.

As dads, we discipline not merely from our position of authority, but primarily out of love. We can be the authority without being authoritarian. We can discipline without being a strict and harsh disciplinarian. Though both approaches may curb or even correct behavior, only one can really touch the heart.

Plato wrote, "Of all the animals, the boy is the most unmanageable." And being the dad of a boy can be a classic case of Man vs. Wild. But we want to avoid the extremes of exercising either too little or too much discipline. Don't overdo it. Always make the penalty fit the crime. Be fair and use common sense. Don't be Policeman Dad, always looking for something to correct or discipline. That will create fear, anxiety, and most of all, distance between the two of you. Instead, always affirm your love for your son without lessening his discipline. Remember, there's a time for mercy too, and sometimes giving him grace when he has disobeyed can touch his heart faster and deeper than a swat on the bottom or grounding him.

As your son grows, you will grow in your understanding of how to discipline him. And you'll need some serious cash in that relationship trust account for those times. For discipline during your son's teenage years you'll have to rely on words of correction, withholding privileges, taking away certain items like the gaming system, computer, iPod, phone, car. But your son needs to understand that you're still the boss, even if he's outgrowing you physically. Again, he may provide you with good behavior if you demand it, but *respect* is something that must be earned by you. Let him know where the boundaries are and communicate them clearly.

The manner of discipline may change, but the principle doesn't. And depending on the boy, you may have very little about which to correct him. That still doesn't mean he won't need your guidance and advice. Remember, this is his first time around in life. He doesn't have the perspective that comes from years of living, learning, growing, and recovering from past mistakes and failures like you do.

That's why you need wisdom from above when it comes to discipline.

That same wise man Solomon also wrote the following advice for dads like you and me:

A youngster's heart is filled with foolishness, but physical discipline will drive it far away.

—Proverbs 22:15 NLT

Do not withhold discipline from a child; if you punish him with the rod, he will not die.

—Proverbs 23:13

Physical discipline may well save them from death.

—Proverbs 23:14 NLT

To discipline a child produces wisdom, but a mother is disgraced by an undisciplined child.

—Proverbs 29:15 NLT

Applying loving discipline, even if you have a strong relationship with your boy, still isn't easy, but it almost always pays off in a young man who has a measure of self-control and can accept responsibility for himself. That will pay off for him, too, and when all is said and done, he'll thank you for it.

Stability

Having worked with many young men over the years, I can tell you that stability is one of the things they desire most in a dad. Can you imagine arriving home from work each day, not knowing whether your house would be there? Think of how uncertain your life would be if, when you got to work tomorrow, you didn't know if you'd have a job. What if you lived every day that way? How crazy would that be, and what a way to live your life? Just like you need a certain degree of predictability in your life as an adult, so your son does in his. By predictable here I don't mean mundane or boring. Life with boys rarely is. But what a boy craves is a predictable relationship environment. And one he can understand. One he can depend on. One he can count on to be secure. That means dad is the same dad each day to him. It means your son doesn't get Angry Dad one day and Fun Dad the next. It means Dad possesses emotional stability, a character quality that usually spills over into junior's life too.

This means Dad works hard at arriving home at about the same time each night. Or at least the family understands why Dad has to be gone. But at the same time, a father needs to learn the skill of leaving his job at the office. Stability for your son means you are emotionally there for him, not hiding behind the newspaper or in front of a TV or computer screen. It means you're available and accessible. It's understandable that sometimes you just can't be there. Like the other night when my son called at midnight to inform his mom he'd run out of gas—and no, there wasn't a date with him. I was out of town on a speaking engagement and couldn't help him, so Mom had the unfortunate task of climbing out of bed and doing the job I would have done. But even then, he knew somebody would be there for him.

Someone always has been.

Your son must know that he can call Dad when he's had a wreck or done something stupid and needs help. It's in those moments he'll find out what's really important to his daddy. And hearing that reassuring voice on the other end of his cell phone will make him feel secure and know all is well. He'll feel stable and sure that his world isn't crumbling around him.

And the benefits of this constancy in his life? A secure boy isn't easily influenced by the crowd. He doesn't feel the urge to verbally put down others because he's already secure in who he is. He doesn't have to overachieve academically or socially in order to prove himself to others. A boy who grows up secure generally doesn't feel the need to fill his life with drugs, deviant behavior, or unhealthy relationships with girls. That's because his emotional tank has already been filled with a secure feeling nurtured by a stable dad.

Our sons enjoy stability as an overflow of our own lives, character, and homes we are building. And here's another way wisdom builds a house.

Family

The family is an endangered species in our culture. Even the concept of family has been the subject of heated debate in our time. What exactly is a family? And is it limited to the traditional model of the two-parent, happily married couple with Dad as the sole provider and his wife as the ever-dutiful stay-at-home Mom? Is that it? Maybe. Maybe not. Most of our marriages are far from perfect, and necessity dictates that Mom may have to pull in some income as well. That's reality. There are also a lot of single-parent or divided-parent families in which both Dad and Mom are struggling to bring a sense of family into their son's life. Perhaps you're one of them. If so, don't despair.

There are all kinds of views regarding family in our culture. And not just in the world "out there," but also in the Christian community. Some people have taken the concept so far as to morph family and church into one, and have no real connection in a local church. That's a bit odd to me. And there are other strange views concerning this awesome organic institution God created. Some people turn family into a sort of cultlike experience in which *everything* is about family. Nothing happens outside the family. Children aren't allowed outside the home for secular events, school, movies, sleep-overs with friends, youth group trips, dates, or sporting events. And the only time the kids are free to do stuff outside the home is when they're doing it with other kids whose parents have the same philosophy. It's like the parents are trying to create a whole other subculture. But as history, society, and even the Bible have taught us, those experiments never really work. Rent the movie *The Village* if you have any doubts.

Kids in these environments have no real individual identity, and their whole lives are basically spent helping at home as sort of house slaves, or worse, being given Mom's responsibility of raising the younger siblings. The parents justify this system by pointing out that in the 1800s kids had to get up every day and help run the farm—plow fields, feed chickens, milk cows, gather wood, sew clothes, and so on. But last time I checked, most of us don't live on farms. And none of us live in the nineteenth century. As a result, these kids, raised as if in another time, never develop their own identity before God, which ultimately creates an impersonal and distant view of Him.

My wife was once approached by one of these moms who was considering having all their kids sleep with her and her husband in a family bed. I'm not kidding—this really happened. Shocked, Beverly told her in no uncertain terms that that was the weirdest thing she'd ever heard.

Okay, those are some pretty bizarre examples, but it begs the question, What *does* it mean to create a sense of family? And why is that so important to your son and your relationship to him? How can you as a dad help develop a strong sense of family, and what will that do for your boy? First, make the family a priority. This may sound obvious, but most of us don't erect twelve-foot walls around the house in order to establish a family compound where no one can leave without proper paperwork. Most families don't spend twenty-four hours a day together. Instead, most of us struggle to find the time for family. And the older your kids get, the harder it becomes. That's why you have to make the time. Schedule it. Plan for it. Steal it. Barter for it. Log it into your digital calendar, because if you don't, something else will fill that slot. Guaranteed.

We all have to work and devote a certain amount of allegiance to our jobs and careers. That's a given. But once the work day is done, you have to make home *the* priority. There is a newly married young man in our church who is a professional golfer. In his twenties, Luke is an amazing athlete, and very good at what he does. Luke and I meet with a small group of men every Tuesday morning to talk about God, life, and how we can support and encourage each other. When Luke talks about his schedule and what he's doing that week, he usually talks about golf. Practicing golf, traveling to play golf, getting golf lessons from another professional, or playing in a tournament. Luke is very good at golf because at this time in his life, golf is a huge priority. And what's true for golfers is also true for dads.

Sociologically speaking, a family is a sort of *people group*. And as such, it will develop its own sense of identity. Helping your family have that identity is one of the greatest things you can do for them and for your son. Everyone craves identity. Everyone wants to feel wanted, loved, important, and a part of a people group. That's why you see kids wearing athletic jerseys. They're identifying themselves with that team or player. That's why teenagers dress goth, or prep, emo, redneck, gangsta, hip hop, or conservative. They want to be identified with something cool and with something that makes them feel good about themselves. That's okay. God put that longing into each one of us. And it's an irresistible desire that, one way or another, will be fulfilled. But your son's sense of family can also help shape a healthy sense of identity for him.

So give him something to work with. Tell him about his family history. Dust off the old photos of your ancestors, telling stories about what you know of them. Better yet, let his grandparents do it. Watch old home movies—and laugh. Visit graveyards. Take him back to the house where you grew up. Help him understand his connection to the past. Let him know where his roots are. Visit relatives often. Make a connection with grandparents, aunts, uncles, and cousins. Trace your family history. Make a family tree. Celebrate your racial heritage or ethnicity. Your boy should know where he came from. It's a part of what has shaped who you are and plays a part in shaping how he sees himself.

And it's okay if your extended family has a somewhat colorful past. Most families do, they just don't talk about it. I had a friend years ago who was rummaging around in her attic and came across a police mug shot . . . of her *dad!* Surprised and confused, she brought the photo down to her father and asked about it. An older man by this time, "Pam's" father explained to his ten-year-old daughter that he had once been an outlaw back in the 1930s, and that, in fact, he was the only surviving member of the Bonnie and Clyde gang! Talk about a revelation!

Maybe your family isn't quite so . . . um . . . interesting, but there will come an appropriate time when junior will need to know that Uncle Frank spent some time in the Big House or that Aunt Jill struggles with alcohol. And there will also come a time when he'll need to hear *your* story as well. A while back I told my three sons the real story behind my conversion to Christianity. They'd heard the

G-rated version I'd delivered to students while speaking at camps and conferences. And they'd seen my wild hippie photos. But they'd never heard the rest of the story. So I sat them down in the kitchen a few years ago and unveiled the PG-13 rendition of the Jeff Kinley Story, complete with my drug abuse, lawbreaking escapades, and near-death experiences. After concluding the detailed version of how I came into a relationship with God, my middle son Stuart sheepishly raised his hand.

"Dad," he said hesitantly, "you never killed anybody, did you?"

Hey, it's your family and your story. So tell it to your son.

What this sense of history does is give your son a sense of belonging. That's why you should always celebrate birthdays. Always. And create your own unique family traditions. Do stuff that fits you and your son. Early on, our stuff was wrestling. Every night following dinner, I took on three eager young boys in the hallway, covering myself with a blanket and pretending to be the dreaded Tickle Monster or challenging them in a game of indoor one-on-three football.

Occasionally we'd go camping, either individually or as a family. At first we just camped in the back yard. I ran a hundred-foot extension cord out to the tent so we could watch cartoons and Three Stooges movies all night. Breakfast was McDonald's.

I am *such* an outdoorsman.

Later on, our tradition became Friday Night at the Movies. We ate popcorn and cheese dip and watched lots of action and adventure movies . . . *guy* movies. Then came high-school football and those Friday nights got moved to Saturday. Now my oldest and I share significant time around the fire pit in the back yard and talk about the stuff that really matters in life.

All these activities have helped establish some real "guy traditions" in the Kinley family. My boys and I shoot guns together, and when we're visiting my family in South Carolina, all ten Kinley boys take their guns out into the woods where we shoot at targets. It's quite a spectacle to see ten handguns fire at once, and testosterone fills the forest air. My boys and I have always had fun, enjoyed each other's company, and laughed . . . a lot.

But the tradition stuff isn't really about the activity as much as it's about the chance to bond with your son while doing something together. Something *he* likes. It means once again, you are in *his* world. That doesn't mean you have to coach every sports team he's on. Neither does it mean you should *never* help out.

I realize it may be somewhat easier to establish a manly identity with your son when you have an all-boy family. Having girls is another subject altogether, a book I'm not qualified to write, though many of the same wisdom principles apply. The big idea is to create a sense of belonging and family by doing stuff together—trips, vacations, lunches, Super Bowl parties, hunting, watching TV, campouts, backyard baseball, skiing . . . and just hanging out.

But know that as your son grows older and develops more into his own person, this family identity won't be quite as critical as it once was. Don't panic. During his teenage years, God will move him to begin establishing his own identity. He needs to know he's okay outside the home, so you'll have to give him opportunities to experience what it's like out there.

In reality, this independence happens little by little all along. You don't just drop him off at college one day and hope he survives. But starting with the first time you deposit him at the church nursery, he begins learning how to relate and cope, using the skills you've developed in your relationship with him. All along, he learns to relate to people who are different from him and his family. He learns to process authority, respect others, and share. But it's at home, with you and those who make up your family, that he learns how to live, love, forgive, and sacrifice.

All in the family.

Encouragement. Discipline. Stability. Family. Four pillars, four solid foundation posts sunk deep into the ground. These form the foundation for your own personal clubhouse, the *Manhut* for you and your boy. They serve as a root system like no other. These are the things that help forge the bond, creating that "special place" in your relationship with him. And they will be the foundation, the roots that will hold your relationship together during the tough times. Life may

shake you. Even test you. But it won't blow you away. Your relationship with your son will stand strong and survive (see Matt. 7:24–25).
Like a massive oak tree in a hurricane.

CHAPTER 7

Hotties and Home Girls

Tammy was my first real heartthrob. My very first crush. We met on the grade-school playground one day and it was, as they say, love at first sight. Yeah, she was pretty, but whatever . . . she could also kick a kickball a country mile—a plus when choosing a fifth-grade girlfriend. After a brief courtship during which I won her affections because I could kick the same ball over the playground fence, I decided to pop the proverbial question to her. But to make it official I'd first, of course, have to purchase the ring.

And so, walking the half-mile down Main Street to the local K-Mart, I strutted up to the jewelry counter and began browsing rocks. After passing on lesser stones, I eventually landed on one, after which I dug into my pockets and pulled out a whopping $1.79. This mother lode of cash enabled me to buy the prettiest piece of cut glass ever set into a band of fake gold-colored metal.

Securing my precious gem in a safe place for a few days, I was finally ready to do the deed. So I strolled the three blocks from my house to hers, and ceremoniously presented it to her in the sunroom of her home. Pleasantly surprised, Tammy accepted my proposal and we officially became boyfriend and girlfriend.

This called for a celebration, so I took her to the movies. Mom drove us. It was a double feature actually—*War of the Gargantuas* and *Monster Zero*. Two low-budget, sci-fi movies portraying men in rubber dinosaur suits fighting each other in slow motion over miniature cities. Classic. And I loved it, especially when she squeezed my hand during the scary parts. Two weeks later, however, Tammy walked up to me before school one day and announced unexpectedly that we were over.

"Over?" I said with a quizzical look blanketing my freckled face.

She then placed the ring back into my hand. Shocked and dismayed, I stood there frozen and speechless as she nonchalantly walked away. I just couldn't accept the fact that we were indeed over. I felt cast aside like a candy wrapper. How could this be? We were an item. We had only just begun. This scenario was definitely *not* in the plan. And as my ten-year-old heart shattered onto the grade-school sidewalk, I shook my head in confusion, and formed my first solid conclusion about the female of the species.

Girls are weird.

You know what I'm talking about, don't you? Girls are simply not like us, something we discover after spending about five minutes with them. They think differently. Act differently. Respond differently. Feel differently. And most of what they say doesn't even make much sense. It does to other girls, though. They totally get it. They communicate to each other with looks, words, and sounds unfamiliar to the male creature. It's like girls are a sci-fi genre all their own, only they're anything *but* low budget! And when they cry—which they do very well—we try to be sensitive by asking them what's wrong, and they say, "Nothing." Go figure. But tragically, Tammy and I never even got to that wonderful stage of the relationship. And I never found out why she rejected me.

That was a long time ago, and there were other girlfriends to follow. And today I still hold to my belief that girls are weird. I have to. I'm a guy. I have to uphold the ideals of my gender. But though that was one of the first lessons I ever learned about girls, it certainly wasn't the last. I soon discovered that in addition to being weird, girls could also be . . . shall we say . . . hot. Very hot. No—make that *smoking* hot.

It didn't take me long to figure out that in spite of their obvious conflicting differences, guys and girls went together very well, like in a natural way. I mean, my buddy Bruce was fun to play guitar with, and Ricky and I played a lot of baseball together. But I never wanted to kiss them! Tammy, however, was a different story. It became apparent to me from an early age that the subject of females would be an interesting study for me.

Or series of studies.

Growing up like most kids, I was a product of my culture. A boy-sized lump of clay easily molded by his surroundings. So it stands to reason that my view of girls and women was largely shaped by my culture and its values. But that's nothing new. For centuries, in fact since time began, women have been at the mercy of cultural values, and for centuries suffered under the mistreatment of men. I think that state of affairs primarily has something to do with guys being typically bigger and stronger than girls. And because we're basically selfish ogres driven by our desire to conquer and dominate stuff, we mistreat women with our attitudes and actions.

Throughout history, women have been seen by men as objects. Specifically, objects of lust, which is a strong, compelling sexual desire. You can be pretty sure the teenage boys over at the local high school rarely struggle with viewing women as house cleaners, baby makers, and chefs. Instead, those boys are most often drawn to those girls in a sexual way. And to some degree that's a natural thing, but we'll talk about that in the next chapter. No skipping ahead to the juicy parts!

For now, it's important for us to understand *why* we think of girls this way and ultimately why we treat them like sex objects. It's also important to confess that this view is wrong. Period. Meaning it misses God's intended design for guy-girl relationships. We also have to recognize the inherent roles that have been assigned to women. Some of them good and some of them not so good.

Eve of Destruction?

In the beginning, there was a strategy and design to the creation of girls. If you recall, God made the first two people, male and female. Though He made us with some common human similarities, God also equipped us with some differences. That's okay. It's supposed to be that way. That's just part of the plan. If you believe the creation story as told in the Bible—and there aren't any good reasons not to—God scraped up some dirt and made a man, promptly naming him *Adam*. Then at some unspecified time He put Adam under supernatural anesthesia, took out one of his ribs, and made a woman. Dirt and ribs. Odd materials from which to craft a species. From the beginning it was easy to notice the physical differences of size, strength, skin, bone structure, reproductive organs—and figure out the differences in body chemistry, hormones, emotions, and even DNA.

I suspect that before they disobeyed God, Adam and Eve understood each other pretty well, appreciating those unique qualities in one another. No arguing, bickering, complaining, or nagging in the garden of Eden. There was harmony in the creation song, and the whole human race (population: 2) got along perfectly with one another.

But once that dissonant, disobedient chord was struck, things went south pretty quick. Instead of complimenting his wife, Adam now blamed Eve for the biggest mistake ever made on earth. She in turn blamed the snake, and the snake . . . well, he had nobody to pin this thing on so he just slithered away. Instead of harmony, there was now hate as the firstborn son of humanity eventually killed his younger brother. We're talking murder! And there were only a few people wandering around the neighborhood! By this point in the story, Adam no longer understood his wife the way God intended him to. For the first time, he had to work at it.

And we guys have been working at it ever since . . . with not much success.

The ensuing rape, murder, and carnage that marked humanity's infant history was only slightly slowed down by a universal flood, which wiped out everybody except eight people. And today we're not much more civilized in our world, considering that abuse, injustice, and mistreatment of women continues throughout the nations—some of it through violence and some through social, political, or even religious oppression.

But though we're still paying the price for that original selfishness in the garden, all is not lost. The game isn't over. There is hope. Hope that first came walking out of Nazareth in carpenter's sandals.

The "Elevator"

Most people don't think of Jesus as a pioneer for women's rights. He's not generally known for His liberation of women. Savior. Son of God. Teacher. But, Women's Rights Advocate? No, it's not usually in the top five names we use to describe Him. And He doesn't get many props for it, either. But actually, Jesus introduced a new and radical code of values regarding women. You have to understand that Jesus grew up in a culture that saw women as second-class citizens at best. But He challenged the status quo of His day. He dared to confront the existing sexist customs regarding divorce, which in His day allowed a husband to get rid of his wife for something as trivial as burning dinner!

Can you see that in some ancient court of law? "Your honor, my client is filing for divorce. I'd like to introduce Exhibit A—this burnt pork chop!"

One time in first-century Israel, a woman was caught by some men in the act of adultery. I don't even want to know *how* they did this. Then they dragged her before Jesus to see what He would recommend for her punishment. Would it be stoning, which is what the Jewish law required for such a crime? Or would He give her mercy, in which case Jesus would be seen as soft on sin? Quite a predicament for the self-proclaimed Messiah. But being a Master of reason and wisdom, Jesus turned the tables on those men by responding, "If any one of you is without sin, let him be the first to throw a stone at her" (John 8:7).

And one by one, each man dropped his stones and walked away. And the woman was instantly elevated.

In virtually every recorded encounter of Jesus and a woman, He broke tradition and violated the customs and laws of His day. How radical Jesus must have been! As far as we know, He only told two people that they had great faith—and one of them was a non-Jewish woman (see Matt. 15:21–28). Did you know that it was women who financially underwrote the ministry of Jesus, making it possible for the disciples to travel, eat, and lodge (see Luke 8:3)? And these loyal female followers of Christ were there at the cross, following Him all the way to the end. Risking ridicule, imprisonment, and even death, they were not ashamed to be publicly identified with Him. Meanwhile, the male disciples were back home, shivering under the covers!

Some of these women were the first to see Jesus risen from the dead (see John 19:25; 20:11–17). Do you see a message here? A pattern? This clearly demonstrates how Jesus viewed women in the context of an oppressive culture.

One day my wife and I received a phone call from a teacher at school who informed us that our oldest son, Clayton, in fifth grade at the time, had called a female classmate a certain colorful name that rhymes with *witch*. Surprised as you might imagine, we confronted Clayton when he got home from school. It went down like this.

DAD: Son, did you call Brook a b—— today at school?
CLAYTON: Sir? No, sir! What does that word mean?
DAD: That's not important right now. What's important is that you tell the truth to your mom and dad.
CLAYTON: But Dad, I didn't call her that. Promise. I don't remember saying *anything* to her.

So Bev and I did some investigative work, trying to get to the bottom of the story. Turns out that this girl, a somewhat pudgy prima donna, had strutted up to Clayton in the line after recess and demanded to cut in line in front of him. The eleven-year-old diva then proceeded to shove Clayton down with such force that he landed pretty hard on his bottom, scraping his elbows. Embarrassed and bleeding in front of his fellow classmates, he got angry and let out his famous utterance.

Not much was said that evening as we tried to contact some more eyewitnesses to this event. But the following morning, Clayton came barreling down the stairs to breakfast.

"Mom! Dad! I remember now. I remember what I said. Laying back on the ground with my elbows all scraped up and bleeding, I yelled, 'Brook, you're such a PIG!'"

Aha.

And so this portion of the puzzle was solved. Thankful he wasn't cussing out girls at school, Clayton had still degraded Brook by using abusive language—and you can debate amongst yourselves whether or not his verbal assault fit her crime. Nevertheless, Clayton had mistreated her, and there was now some restitution to make. So after some Mom-Dad consultation, we came up with a plan we felt good about. First, we asked him to pick up the phone and call Brook's dad, who by this time had caught wind of the famous B-word name-calling. You can imagine how intimidating it is for a young boy to call a girl's dad. But dutifully, Clayton faced up to this "man moment" with courage, phoning her dad and asking his forgiveness for insulting his daughter. The poor guy had no idea how to respond, and there was an extended pause of awkward silence on the other end of the phone.

Then we also asked Clayton to withdraw money from his stash and go buy flowers for Brook, personally delivering them to her front door, which he did in great humility. This was accompanied by an apology, after which she snatched the flowers out of his hand and disappeared back inside, slamming the door in his surprised face. But it didn't matter what her response was. What mattered was that Clayton did the right thing.

And he learned a valuable lesson about how *not* to treat the opposite sex.

Though not enamored with girls like his dad was in the fifth grade, Clayton still needed to develop a view of women that included refraining from hurling insults. Instead we wanted him to learn how to honor them with his attitudes and actions. And to learn when to simply walk away without a word.

I think Jesus would have been happy with that, because He treated women with unusual equality and dignity, elevating their status far above what any religious leader or rabbi had done previously. I think that's because Jesus knows something about girls and women that we also need to know. For one, He knows they make great Christ-followers and are able to lead others to do the same. He also knows they have a vital contribution to make to the human race. He understands that in many areas they can do things men typically can't do, and that they are uniquely gifted and qualified in areas such as organization, administration, loyalty, and discernment. Women can also multitask well, and tend to be excellent communicators. But beyond just knowing all these things about women, Jesus demonstrated His attitude about them by showing that girls are made by God and have unlimited worth in His eyes.

That's what Jesus thinks of women.

Maybe we should think that way too.

Home Girls

It's one thing, having to put up with all kinds of girls at school—even girls who push you down. But where the rubber really meets the road is at home. The way a boy grows up, treating his mom and sisters, says a great deal about him as a person. That's because home, like no other place, is where we really learn to love, sacrifice, and forgive. Family relationships are where our boys develop the mind-set and skills necessary to overcome our culture's twisted ideas and practices. Part of this development is simply being sensitive to their moms. One writer of Scripture referred to a husband's responsibility to his wife this way: "Husbands, in the same way be *considerate* as you live with your wives, and treat them with *respect* as the weaker partner and as heirs with you of the gracious gift of life, so that nothing will hinder your prayers" (1 Peter 3:7, emphasis added).

Considerate respect.

That's a great phrase. And a good guide when thinking about girls. What an excellent model for a young man to follow when forming his opinion of girls at home and relating to them. What female wouldn't like a guy who is considerate and respectful toward her? The Bible also has something to say to women, of course, about how they ought to treat their husbands, but perhaps a woman should write *that* book. The apostle Peter's idea here was that, in light of the fact that women are weaker, we should treat them accordingly. With gentleness and sensitivity.

Considerate respect.

Obviously girls are not weaker intellectually or spiritually, but they are still generally more fragile than we are. They typically lean on us, not vice versa. We provide a stability for them they don't get from other women. That's part of our role in their lives. This means we realize they are not as hardened or tough as we are, and that our words to them and physical treatment have to be tempered and scaled back in light of this.

It's like the difference between tackling a guy your own size in the back yard and tackling your best friend's five-year-old son. With your buddy, you're trying to cause some hurt. Maybe clean his clock or knock him into another time zone. But with the five-year-old, you naturally use more tact, finesse, control. And why? So you don't break the little guy in half! And just because he's smaller or younger doesn't make him inferior to you or less important. It's just the opposite. His smaller size and weaker state causes you to use self-restraint, becoming more purposeful as you gently tackle him on the grass.

I'm not proposing that you tackle your wife, but I am suggesting that how you treat her will set a visible standard for your son. He will subconsciously look to you for that informal training. And this is one standard that will be tested more and more as he grows older, more physically mature and independent. He'll likely begin talking back to his mom sometime during prepuberty. The "yeah" or "what?" instead of "yes, ma'am" is one of the signs. Over time and with his growth, Mom doesn't seem so big to him anymore. And in a boy's mind, bigger always wins over smaller. You have to reverse that thinking by your words and actions.

Also, as your son develops physically, he'll experience hormonal changes that will likely cause him to be more aggressive, verbally and physically. That's why guys like to wrestle and make fun of each other. We also do this because, of course, we're insecure. But as this aggressiveness increases, he'll need an outlet for this emotion and energy through physical activities like sports, during which he can blow off some steam in healthy ways. That's why football is so good for boys. Again, where else in life do you get to knock the snot out of some poor guy, and hundreds of people stand to their feet in applause?

But this outlet doesn't have to be sports. Just having good fun doing stuff with other guys can be a great way to expend this energy. When this doesn't happen, he takes it out on Mom with his attitudes and words. And why? Because his physical and intellectual development causes him to see her as the weaker vessel. And that inherent male desire to dominate, conquer, and control starts rising to the surface. He senses he is now physically stronger than her, and thinks he's smarter. In his mind, Mom began taking stupid pills just prior to his adolescence. Ha! If he only knew!

That's where you come in, Dad. Your son needs to know what's happening in his body, but he also must understand the consequences of mistreating the girls who live under a common roof. Not only do you model that considerate respect for your son, but you also discipline him like a good coach with the pros and cons of treating her that way. When you do that, he can know what the boundaries are. When each of my boys reached the stage where they started questioning Mom's wisdom, talking back to her with disrespectful words or attitudes, I sat down with them one by one and said:

"Son, here's something you should know. Your happiness over the next six to seven years will be in direct proportion to the way you treat your mother, who also happens to be my wife. I knew her before you were born, and I'll be with her long after you're gone. So if you choose to dis her, know that I'll make it my mission to make your life miserable. Are we clear?"

Now that may sound a bit harsh, but keep in mind, a boy many times needs firm and loving direction. Not abusive, harsh, or overbearing, but *direct*. Eye to eye. Remember, you've already gone through your own adolescent thing. But this is his first time around, so he needs your guidance here. In reality, I expected my sons to respond to those fatherly words of warning, and for the most part, they have. Because I'd spent many years making regular deposits in our relationship trust account, I could speak those words without them thinking me too harsh.

Your son has to recognize, though, that people won't always treat *him* with honesty and fairness. Sister. Brother. Mom. Even Dad. They won't always hit the mark with your son. But it's always easy to treat others with dignity when they also treat us that way, right? Jesus said it's a no-brainer to love those who love you (see Matt. 5:46–47). Anybody can do that. But in the boot camp of home is where respectful attitudes toward women are forged in your son's mind and heart. It's a reality that he'll be challenged with relating to females the rest of his life—classmates, girlfriends, teachers, teammates, neighbors, coworkers, church members, a wife, perhaps a daughter, and yes . . . a mother-in-law. There's just no escaping it. Girls are here to stay. So it seems like a pretty good idea for us men to develop the heart and life skills necessary for maximizing our relationships with them.

Worth and dignity. Considerate respect. These are the lenses through which we want our sons to see girls and women. That's how God sees them. And lining our hearts up with His—isn't that our ultimate life goal?

Cultivating this gentlemanly spirit is one lost art worth rediscovering. If we can help our sons do that, then they'll be able to recognize and resist the negative cultural values when faced daily with them. Showing him this better way may not keep him from getting his heart broken or avoiding the occasional female weirdness, but it will give him courage to do the right thing the next time a girl pushes him down on the playground.

CHAPTER 8

Taming the Lion

Most every creature in the animal kingdom has a natural predator. For the wildebeest of Africa's Serengeti region, it's the lion. The Big Cat. And here's a fun fact: an adult lion can grow to nine feet in length and weigh up to four hundred pounds, needing around fifteen pounds of meat each day to survive. And the meat the lion survives on is the more vulnerable members of the kingdom that live and migrate in that area. Making up about 47 percent of the lions' diet, the wildebeest is at the top of the lion's menu. And while this member of the caribou family can run at speeds up to fifty miles per hour, the lion can reach them before they achieve that speed, usually catching its prey within a few yards. Plus, the wildebeest's horns are no real defense against the stronger lion, especially considering that the wildebeest is usually running in the opposite direction.

If you've ever watched an encounter between these two wild animals on TV, you know it's not a pretty sight. It's surprising to some that the female lioness does most of the hunting for the pride. Not too much smaller than her male counterpart, she stealthily stalks her unsuspecting prey, lying in wait for an opportune time. Then when the angle of attack is right, she leaps out of the bush without warning to pounce on the unfortunate creature. In doing so, she sinks her razor-sharp claws in to the hindquarters of the animal. Stunned, the wildebeest tries to get away, but it's too late. The lion widens its jaws to clamp down on the wildebeest's back with pressure of almost seven hundred pounds per square inch, more force than that of a shark bite. The captured prey jerks and squirms to escape, giving him a false sense of hope. But it's short-lived, for the lion quickly takes a second bite, this one much deeper.

Replanting her claws, she now anchors herself deeper than fur and flesh, penetrating to the tendons and even bone. Dragged down to the dusty Serengeti floor, the wildebeest flashes a look of panic in its eyes, a look that soon turns to resignation. That's when the lion goes for the kill, clamping its jaws like a steel trap on the animal's neck. Following a few final jerks and quivers, the wildebeest succumbs to a violent, painful, yet relatively quick death.

By this time the lioness has been joined by several of her female friends as they begin tearing flesh from bone. After they feed for hours, all that's left behind is the rotting carcass, a benevolent offering for the vultures and smaller animals to eat.

But the lion is not evil for stalking, attacking, and eating the wildebeest. It is simply obeying its instincts, following the ways of nature.

Changes

You and I have a natural predator too. An enemy so inclined to kill and destroy that it knows no other way. Guided by its instincts, it exists to murder. It thrives on catching you off guard, waiting patiently for just the right time to pounce on you and tear you apart. The enemy I'm referring to is the Devil. When the apostle Peter tried to think of the most dangerous word-picture of his day in describing this evil being, God led him to use the imagery of a lion. Had you lived in first-century Palestine, there would have been no more terrifying a thought than to be attacked by a lion. Peter warns us of the Devil's nature and mission—prowling, looking, and then devouring (see 1 Peter 5:8). He loves to devour.

This Devil is a real spiritual entity. He's not a made-up character, some cartoon figure or a fictional nemesis manufactured to scare you. And he's also not some impersonal force. He's real. Very real. His existence is, in fact, surer than any physical enemy you or I could have. The physical world we live in is, after all, only temporal; the spiritual world goes on forever. So as he's done since before Adam and Eve, the

Devil lives to steal, kill, and destroy (see John 10:10). This Devil isn't random or indiscreet in his hunt for prey. Not at all. He has developed an acute taste for humans, and nothing less will do. But it's not just any human he hunts. He wants *your* blood . . . yours and your son's.

This Devil has many strategies to destroy. He enjoys pouncing on you, penetrating your spirit with anger, apathy, or—one of his personal favorites—pride. He plays on our insecurities, anxieties, and fears, capitalizing on anything that threatens our progress toward true manhood. He plays up to our masculinity because he knows we crave to be masculine. All of us men desperately want to be cool, in control, secure, and most of all, loved.

But one of his preferred targets is in the arena of our sexual desires, commonly called lust. The Devil has a unique skill of taking a God-given desire and perverting it into a craving, obsession, or addiction that can consume us. This perversion of sexual desire also has some of its roots in the values of the culture in which we live. And during the season we call *puberty* and the time leading up to it, your son is experiencing a world of change; change that impacts his interaction with his sexuality. This change is a time-released metamorphosis encoded by God at your son's conception and that unfolds during the preadolescent and teen years. And once puberty begins, things start changing in a boy's body, sometimes rapidly and other times more gradually.

Mental changes: Up to this point, your son's mental abilities have largely been limited to concrete thoughts, but during puberty he'll be able to dialogue more intelligently about subjects and philosophical concepts that were generally out of his reach prior to this time. The good side of this development is that you'll be able to have some cool discussions with him about things you're both interested in. The down side is that he may out-think you from time to time!

Emotional changes: Your boy's emotions also will be affected by puberty. He may experience outbursts of anger or occasional uncontrolled aggression. He may also begin communicating with a series of grunts and groans, more resembling a prehistoric caveman than the precious son you once knew. You might even catch him shedding a tear in sorrow, anger, or frustration from time to time. But don't panic. As he grows, he'll likely rediscover the English language and rejoin humanity.

Social changes: The art of growing as a person involves the increased capacity to experience relationship. And because your son grows socially, he'll become more aware of himself and his identity. He instinctively wants to know who he is, and that discovery may mean he tries on various hats during this time. Depending on the circle of friends he's drawn to, his style of dress may change several times. Or his music. Even his friends may rotate. Now, more than ever, his search for significance kicks in. He will experiment with identity, so you will have to guide him through this time. Your track record of unconditional love and acceptance will be invaluable during this time.

A note here: Helping your boy choose his friends early on in life can positively influence his own choice of them later in adolescence. His involvement in the area of friends may reflect unhealthy extremes. On one end of the spectrum his friends are everything and 100 percent of his social identity is derived from who his friends are. On the other end, he may become a complete recluse with no social contact at all. This isolation will warp him and retard his social growth and his ability to relate and interact with people later on. A third extreme is when he chooses unhealthy friends who will influence him in negative ways. All these extremes are major red flags to you that something big is missing in his life. So get on top of the friend-making process early on. Be proactive.

The fact remains, our sons change during puberty, and we hope they develop and progress positively in these areas.

Oh, I almost forgot one more area of change . . . *physical change*. Puberty brings the release of hormones in a boy, specifically testosterone. This chemical, manufactured by the body, specifically secreted by the adrenal glands and the testes, helps increase his body size, energy, and sexual desire. The effects are many. First, his voice begins changing, taking him from Alvin and the Chipmunks to Darth Vader in a matter of months. This also creates some episodes of voice-cracking at awkward times. You remember doing that in history class, don't you? Also included in the puberty package is pubic hair appearing, along with some facial hair. But don't freak if he can't grow a full beard by the eighth grade. The amount of hair and placement on his face is completely determined by genetics, sometimes from his mother's side of the family. Hair also starts sprouting under his arms, giving him—and you—a reason to invest in the wonderful world of deodorant.

Puberty also produces changes in his genitals, and he begins experiencing an interesting phenomenon—erections. Though this may not be something completely unfamiliar to him, it may start happening involuntarily and at odd times—like at basketball practice or during church. This is perfectly normal, though certainly not convenient. He may also occasionally have a wet dream during which semen is released during the night. This too is normal and something over which he has no control. Let him know ahead of time about these things, so he doesn't think he's a mutant or something. But it's the increasing change regarding his penis that makes him even more curious, increasing his fascination with what that thing between his legs is really for.

And that's where things start to get tricky.

It's a Full Moon

As a young boy, I remember being scared by those old Dracula and Frankenstein movies. Filmed in black and white, they somehow seemed more eerie. But the one that frightened me the most was the Wolfman. This movie told the story of a mild-mannered man named Lawrence Talbot who was bitten by a wolf. Soon afterward, at the appearance of a full moon, Talbot begins a slow transformation into the murderous werewolf—half man, half wolf. The movie uses then-innovative time-lapsed photography to portray the gradual change from man to werewolf—growing hair, longer fingernails, wolves' paws, and sharp, pointy teeth—until finally the transformation is complete. Talbot can help himself no longer. He has no control over his instincts or actions. Deep inside, he really doesn't want this change. He resists. He fights it. But all his efforts are in vain. It's no use. His animal DNA now overrules his human chemistry and decency. He's a werewolf now, and the only thing he can do is kill.

Residing within every boy is the risk that this God-designed thing called puberty can eventually turn on him. A mild-mannered boy can easily become a raging monster of sexual desire unless this area of life is understood and managed. Sometimes the lust monster creeps up on us, surprising us. Without warning. We didn't plan it and we couldn't help it. It just appears, from out of nowhere. Boom! There it is. And its presence is strong. Very strong.

I used to think of sexual lust as a dragon that God wanted us as noble knights to go out and slay. Like a threatening enemy, the best battle plan would be just to kill it, right? Put it to death once and for all. But like all honest men I eventually discovered that my sexual desire wasn't going away. It wasn't going to die. It wasn't supposed to. God put it there. He thought of the idea and put it inside each of us. It's a heavenly gift, not a creation of culture or Hollywood. Our desire to experience sexual fulfillment and intimacy was also put there by our Creator. As Howard Hendricks, one of my seminary professors used to say, "We should never be ashamed to discuss what God was not ashamed to create."

I agree.

There is no shame in discussing the desire for women that God has placed within men. So instead of trying to slay the dragon, I think it's better to view sexual desire as a lion that must be controlled. You can tame a lion, locking him in a protective cage while maintaining a safe distance. Lions are awesome and entertaining that way, even enjoyable. But you always have to keep in mind that they can turn on you at any time. Without warning. We can never turn our backs on a lion while in its presence. In the same way, the sexual urges your son will begin to feel can never be left unchecked or unattended. If not understood, managed, and controlled, the urge will follow its instincts and go straight for the jugular. In short, we have to learn how to sleep with one eye open.

Understanding Lust

So how do we help our sons navigate the tricky currents of this area? May I suggest a couple of ideas? First, talk to him about it. As soon as you think he's ready to handle the subject, take him away somewhere and discuss it. Ask him questions about what he's heard about sex, girls, and even his own body. Yes, it will be awkward. Especially at first. But that's okay. Do it anyway. Once you break the ice, you'll feel better. He may be a little close-lipped about things, so ask open-ended questions that don't require a yes or no answer. But get alone with him on a fishing trip or camping excursion. Take a long drive together. Attend a father-son retreat where the topic of sex is being discussed. Enlist the help of youth leaders or other Christian mentors. But just know that it will eventually mean more when the conversation is driven by dad himself. Just make sure you do it. Do it before he forms ideas and opinions from the guys at school, in the locker room, or worst of all on the Internet.

Secondly, explain to him or remind him about the changes taking place in his body. Talk about sexual temptation, or the desire to look at, or think about, a girl lustfully. Let him know that all men struggle in this area, even you. Explain to him what God says about temptation (see 1 Cor. 10:13). Help him understand that . . .

- It's normal. It happens to everyone. Nobody gets a bye in this contest.
- It occurs regularly. It happens most every day, if not several times a day.
- It's *not* sin. Jesus was tempted, and yet we know He never sinned, so it's not a sin for us to be tempted. Just because you look at a girl and a thought pops into your head doesn't mean you have sinned. It's what you *do* with that thought that really matters.
- It can be overcome. God promises to never let us be tempted with something too big for us to handle with His help.

Talk to your son about lust—what it is and how it works. Help him to understand that to lust after something just means to have a strong desire for it. That desire doesn't have to be wrong or unhealthy. But when it's a strong sexual desire, that's when we have to think about whether it's positive or harmful. Right or wrong. Show him how lust works and what it does to us.

A biblical author put it this way,

> And remember, no one who wants to do wrong should ever say, "God is tempting me." God is never tempted to do wrong, and he never tempts anyone else either. Temptation comes from the lure of our own evil desires. These evil desires lead to evil actions, and evil actions lead to death. So don't be misled, my dear brothers and sisters. (James 1:13–16 NLT)

Many times, our own evil desires are the source of our temptation. Sometimes those desires are conjured up by our sinful minds. And other times they're aroused by other stimuli. We can't always blame culture, the Internet, or girls who wear revealing clothes. The one ultimately to blame is the part of us that enjoys sinning (see Rom. 7:18). But those desires can quickly grow, leading to sinful actions. And those actions lead to death, or a break in the relationship with God.

Desires. Actions. Death.

So what does that look like in the life of a real guy?

Temptation usually begins as a thought in the brain or an attraction through the eyes. As guys, we are stimulated and aroused primarily through eyesight and mental images. That's why 95 percent of visitors to Internet porn sites are men. Sometimes we can't help what passes before our eyes or what images suddenly flash into our brains. But what we *can* control is "Stage Two," which is whether we dwell on those images, turning them into full-length motion pictures in our mind's theater. And if we stay and watch the movie, then "Stage Three" kicks in.

Now we're allowing the desire to grow. And grow it does, like a brushfire. We begin imagining sexual stimulation or taking the steps to turn our fantasy into reality. And that means taking action with our mouths, hands, or penises.

Once we've reached this stage, there's virtually no turning back, and here's why: God *designed* our sexuality to work this way! He made it a natural process for a man to have a strong sexual desire for a woman and to eventually experience sexual fulfillment with her. It's totally cool. Even godly. It's not a question of *if* but when and with whom it happens. Is it within marriage and is it with your wife? According to Scripture, that's the context of godly sexual desire. And He designed those desires to grow to the point of acting on them. And by the time you reach this point, your hormones are raging, your heart is pumping, your mind is racing, and you're feeling something you were meant to feel . . . loved and connected to someone special.

But the question is, Are you connected with that special person or are you simply the victim of your own sexual desire, let out of its cage and into the crowd at the zoo? You see, the thing to keep in mind is that your penis has no idea if you're married or not. It can't make moral choices or healthy decisions. It completely relies on your mind and spirit to guide it to the right time, place, and person. If you get it aroused, it will respond, on cue. Every time. And ultimately where does all this end? It ends in fulfillment. Sexual release. Orgasm. In marriage, this fulfillment is followed by peace and satisfaction. But outside of that relationship it leads to guilt and a host of other unpleasant things. But according to Jesus, it's not just the outward actions we want to prevent. He targeted the attitude of the heart (see Matt. 5:27–28). It's what happens inside our hearts and minds that Jesus is concerned about.

He knows that as the heart and mind go, so go the hands, mouth, and penis. It's as simple as that. God wants us to pursue sexual purity *from the heart.*

Taming the Beast

In order for our sons to gain control of their sexuality, it's important that they know the practical decisions they can make. God would suggest the following game plan:

1. Fill your empty heart (see Ps. 37:4; Eph. 5:18).

Before we can truly understand about controlling sexuality, we have to acknowledge that it's primarily a heart issue. Not a sex problem or a chemical imbalance or a mere bodily function. But a heart thing. A matter of the soul. The reason guys choose to be preoccupied with girls and sex is because of an emptiness of heart.

Hungry men eat. Starving men eat *anything*. But a full stomach is satisfied. When we're empty on the inside the natural tendency is to fill that space. Nature abhors a vacuum. And the nature of man is that he must seek to fill the void inside him. To fill up the space in his heart God desires to fill. Water always flows downhill to the lowest point. When left to ourselves, gravity takes over and we become a thundering torrent, out of control, eventually bursting the dam and flooding our lives with misery. Filling our hearts with unhealthy sexual desire is an attempt to gain satisfaction, fulfillment, significance, and pleasure in something other than the person of God.

Now I have to be brutally honest with you here. Sexual gratification can be very, very satisfying. It feels *good*. It's stimulating. Pleasurable. Erotic. It can feel terrific about a hundred out of a hundred times! We love having orgasms because it *gives* us something, and the benefits are immediate. When we indulge lust, we get instant gratification. Every time. Sin almost always feels good, and right away (Heb. 11:25). But like a drug wearing off, the good feeling soon passes, leaving us empty again, in pain . . .

. . . and feeling guilty.

Bottom line: sex outside God's design is a substitute for the real thing. It's a fake, temporary satisfaction we enjoy, a cheap imitation of what it feels like when Jesus is filling the heart. So because it's primarily a matter of the heart, the best remedy for lust has to be a love relationship with Jesus Christ. The more we are in love with Him, the less likely we will be lured by lust like a fish chasing a spinner. Granted, in the moment, our sexual desires can seem and feel as significant as our pursuit of God. But that's the soul-numbing power of lust at its best, temporarily deadening our spirits like Novocain to a tooth. And when the numbness wears off, the throbbing pain sets in.

Sin makes us stupid.

So to help your boy here, he has to know that God cares first about his heart before his actions. What's in the well always comes up in the bucket. So if the heart is pure, the body will be as well. Focus then on an attitude of daily dependence on Jesus for purity of the heart. Your boy has a choice to make every day whether he will surrender his will to God. To delight himself in Him and not in the counterfeit currency of his own selfish desires. And as he makes this choice, God will strengthen him and begin placing His desires in your boy's heart (see Ps. 37:4). In this way, he can partner with God and develop inner moral integrity. With you there to listen, lead, and encourage, an invisible cord of three strands is woven together—you, your son, and God—and that kind of cord is not easily broken (see Eccl. 4:12).

First, aim for the heart.

2. Guard your mind and eyes (see Job 31:1).

As we saw in the last chapter, our attitude toward women is critical here. But even with a healthy view of the opposite sex, lustful desires can still creep up on us. Since guys are primarily susceptible to sexual temptation through sight, we have to be smart and set a guard over our eyes. Last year, when visiting the United States Military Academy at West Point, we were met at the gate by a soldier. Holding his hand up, he stopped our car and asked for identification. I gave him my driver's license, and he scanned the back of it with a portable, handheld device, which immediately gave him access to everything from a criminal record all the way down to my last parking ticket.

I was clean.

His job is to guard his post, allowing only those with clearance to pass through. Like that sentry at the gate, we have to be alert at all times. Guarding what is allowed into our minds and what passes before our eyes—including movies, magazines, the Internet, and where we go.

Please hear me here. This is in no way an encouragement toward legalism or to suggest removing your son from culture. He will never learn to stand on his own that way. But that also doesn't mean that we indiscriminately allow him to see or be exposed to images that will titillate his libido and arouse his sexual urges.

So what does limiting that experience mean for your boy? You have to make that call yourself, but it may include restricting what TV channels he's allowed to watch, especially early on in life. Managing Internet access is a key area here. The Internet has changed everything—from education to commerce to social networking. And there is unprecedented access to virtually anything imaginable. Today thousands of Internet porn sites are available to your son with just a few clicks of the computer mouse. In a matter of seconds, your son can log on to the most vile and disgusting images ever produced by mankind—from "soft porn" to homosexuality to bestiality. It's everywhere. Pornography is a 97 billion dollar a year industry. Every second, more than three thousand dollars is spent on pornography, and a new porn video is made every thirty-nine minutes.[1]

And it's all easily accessible to your son. So help set a guard at the gate of his mind and heart. You might consider activating parental controls on your computer, or purchasing filtering software or accountability programs such as covenanteyes.com. Preview movies and/or video games he's allowed to see or rent. Again, you're not trying to be legalistic. You're simply guiding your son in how to make wise choices and helping him avoid unnecessary temptation. Eventually, however, he has to be allowed to make his own decisions in this area. And he will make mistakes. Just make sure you're there for him when he does. Helping him mature into manhood means nurturing a mystical sensitivity to God's heart. And that will strengthen him in turning away from worthless and empty pursuits.

His battle, and yours, begins in the mind (Phil. 4:8). It's where images are created, welcomed inside, and ultimately stored forever. You and I both know that things our eyes saw in childhood and adolescence are still there, embedded in our mental memory chip, downloaded and stored in vivid color and high resolution. And these mental pictures are not the kind that fade over time. They're just as colorful and arousing as they were ten, twenty, or thirty years ago.

So with that in mind, we have to guard our minds, not only from what enters into it, but also what is created in it. We can remove ourselves completely from external stimuli and yet still have a fully functioning "lust factory" operating in our brains. That's why we help ourselves win the battle when filling our mind with good things, pure thoughts, and Scripture. Doing so not only replaces those negative influences, but it also trains our minds. It disciplines our minds with "mental muscle memory," helping it to think in healthy ways.

3. Run! (see 2 Tim. 2:22).

When the apostle Paul wrote to young Timothy about this subject, his advice was straightforward and direct: "*Flee* the evil desires of youth, and pursue righteousness, faith, love and peace, along with those who call on the Lord out of a pure heart" (2 Tim. 2:22, emphasis added).

As far as I can tell after almost three decades of studying the Bible, I haven't found one verse that tells me to stand and fight sexual temptation. I mean, what fool would try to take on a charging lion with his bare hands? Paul knows something about sexual temptation that led him to advise Timothy to adopt a strategy of swift retreat. Like fleeing a burning building or running out of the path of an oncoming eighteen-wheeler. Just move! Run! Not hard to understand or complicated. Just get out! Leave! This is the kind of exit strategy that will help your boy stay alive in the battle.

4. Don't walk alone (see Heb. 10:24–25).

Battling with lust can be a lonely experience, primarily because it's somewhat embarrassing to admit to someone else that you struggle in this area. You think you're the only one who has trouble with it. But that's where you're wrong. Lust is every man's struggle. We all face this temptation regularly. No one is exempt. No one is immune. It is a common guy thing. And that's exactly why we so desperately need one another. When we walk alone, we are at our weakest and make ourselves vulnerable to attack. There is strength in numbers, as Solomon wisely observed:

> Two are better than one, because they have a good return for their work: If one falls down, his friend can help him up. But pity the man who falls and has no one to help him up!
>
> Though one may be overpowered, two can defend themselves. A cord of three strands is not quickly broken. (Eccl. 4:9–10, 12)

It's a simple principle worth repeating here. We are stronger when we walk with others on life's journey. That's because there's a fundamental difference between the stability of one and the strength of two. Your son needs the encouragement and accountability of others. And so do you.

Sexual temptation is one enemy we should never face alone. We are outnumbered and outmatched. And the only confidence we can have is knowing that others who love and understand us will stand beside us in this warfare. Too often we're lulled into a false sense of security, thinking, *It won't happen to me.* But that's exactly where the Enemy wants us. That kind of bravado, pride really, is the very thing that will be our downfall. A strong will isn't enough. Having a driven, type A personality won't do it either. Every man has a breaking point, a moment of weakness.

I watched a video on YouTube the other day that showed a family on a photographic safari in Africa. At one point, the dad stepped out of the car to film a pride of lions feasting on the dead carcass of . . . you guessed it . . . a wildebeest. As the man inched closer toward the ravenous lionesses enjoying their meal, the big cats began to snarl at him. But ignoring the growls, the man kept filming, silently making his way closer toward the pride as they tore meat from the dead animal. Then suddenly and unexpectedly, one lioness sprung from her crouching position and pounced on the man, pulling him instantly to the ground. He tried to punch and kick, but it didn't affect the lion one bit.

It was all over in a matter of seconds. As his wife and two small children watched and screamed from the safety of the car, the rest of the pride smelled the blood and joined in on the feast of fresh meat. They began ripping him apart, just like they had done to the wildebeest moments before. Soon, a game warden appeared in a truck and frightened the lions away. But it was too late. This poor dad had literally been eaten alive.

The tragedy of this story lies in the man's failing to recognize he was filming lions on their own turf. He wasn't satisfied with viewing from a distance. Instead, he wanted to see how close he could get. Closer and closer until there was no chance for retreat. No room to run. He ventured in with no backup and no protection. In short, his pride and false sense of security fooled him into thinking the lions wouldn't attack. But they always do.

Lust is like that.

We can look at this man and think how foolish he was for venturing so close. But we do the exact same thing with the lion of lust, don't we? Inching closer and closer, we invite the attack, and lust pounces on us, biting and sinking its teeth deep into our minds and hearts. And if we let this beast walk around our house and heart unchecked, it is sure to attack and kill. As a father, you will have to take the necessary precautions to safeguard your son and yourself from this deadly enemy.

Beware of lions.

CHAPTER 9

The Big Handoff

In a relay race, the most important part is the passing of the baton. This critical exchange must be executed properly for the race to continue. It's the link that ensures the race will carry on to the finish line. This aluminum baton, weighing just a few ounces, must be handed safely from one runner to the next in order for the race to be won.

For those dads who follow Jesus, nothing is more critical than a son's embracing the Christian faith and experiencing a personal relationship with God. But wishing and hoping that your son magically comes to that place in life isn't good enough. It's not enough to simply cheer from the sidelines, believing that by accident or osmosis he will somehow adopt the same beliefs and values as his parents.

Some parents carry the false assumption that because Mom and Dad are Christians, then junior will surely become one too. But in over twenty-five years of working with parents and kids, I've never seen this happen. There is no automatic transfer of faith. And there are no guarantees that your son will embrace faith in God. Honestly, when it comes to our faith, parenting is one of life's greatest gambles. And because this parenting race is a long-distance relay, it requires us to be in a place where endurance and focus converge.

Assuming you've already received the baton of faith from someone else (friend, pastor, parents), your privilege is to now pass it on to the next generation. During your son's childhood years, you alone hold the baton in your hand. As you begin relating to him concerning God, however, he begins to reach out for the baton himself. Then, one day when he's left home, he has the baton himself and is able to pass it along to his children and to his world. It works like this:

Childhood Years	Teenage Years	Adult Years
You have the baton	You both have the baton	He has the baton

You're banking on your own investment in God and in your son, as well as the prayer that your son will see the value and benefits of a life spent in relationship with God. You want him eventually to run his own race. But for that to become reality, several things must happen. The relay race analogy helps us here. For any relay team to complete a race, each runner needs to know what makes a great handoff.

Think about it.

- Both runners have to be in the race, and the first runner has to have the baton. You can't pass on to someone else what you yourself do not possess.
- The first runner has to run toward the second runner. That's the relationship thing we've been talking about in this book.
- The first runner must know how to put the baton squarely into the other runner's hand and not just toss it blindly or flippantly. A purposeful handoff requires wisdom in knowing how faith is processed and passed on.
- The first runner can't expect someone else to hand the baton to the second runner. Some spectator is not going to run out of the stands and do it. Handing down your faith is primarily your responsibility as your son's dad.
- The first runner can't let go until the other runner has completely grasped the baton. Passing along your faith takes time— the entire parenting period—and there are zero shortcuts.
- The second runner has to want the baton for himself, opening his hand and willingly receiving it. The appetite for spirituality and faith is something only God can create, and, again, whetting that hunger is often a long process.
- After receiving the baton, the second runner has to continue

running and not drop it. When it comes to faith, it's easy to trip, become discouraged, and even let go.

• The first runner's role begins to change, now becoming more that of a cheerleader. A dad's part in his son's faith doesn't end when his son becomes a Christian.

Sometimes a dad and son execute a faulty handoff—they fumble the transfer, and the baton is dropped. Some dads simply become tired in the race by the time their boys are teenagers, and the handoff is incomplete. As fathers we can fail to grow and respond properly to each new stage of parenting—to the infant, toddler, child, adolescent. Some dads fall into extremes, and either back off from providing spiritual influence, or bear down too hard on their sons. Both extremes are recipes for disaster.

Keep in mind, though, it's not just *your* faith you're passing down to your boy, but *the* faith. As he embraces a relationship with God, it will not look like a carbon copy of your faith and the way you relate to your Creator. And neither should it. God will have a unique way of revealing Himself to your boy, a way that is relevant and real to *him*. But the bottom line is that you long for him to follow God, right?

With that in mind, I'd like to hand off to you what I've come to believe are some great ideas from God. This wisdom didn't originate with me, so I can't take credit for it. Rather, the following dad-to-dad advice is rooted in Scripture, years of observation, failure, practice, perseverance, and a little common sense. These are not magic formulas that guarantee success. They're not formulas at all. Human life is too complicated and dynamic for trite Christian recipes. Instead, they're simply great ideas that help foster a love relationship between your son and God.

A Good Start

In his childhood, your boy's heart is like wet cement. Impressionable. Easily molded and formed. He has a tender heart and is very teachable. During this period, what you say to him matters.

Everything in life is new to him. New discoveries are happening for him every day. But beyond that, you're his dad—the greatest, coolest, and strongest man ever to walk the earth. That's why early on is the time to begin imprinting him positively with an impression of who God is and how much He loves.

Many men do well during this stage, but remember, anybody can run fifty yards, and anybody can be the doting father for a few years. But we're in a long-distance relay. You can't afford to curb your enthusiasm or allow your sense of vision to diminish as the years pass. In the midst of this often painful race you're in, you can never forget what, and who, you're running for. You can't afford to run well early on, then slack off for years and wait until late in the last lap to attempt a handoff at the last second. The odds of your boy receiving that faith handoff then are slim to none.

The Third Strand

It's primarily your responsibility as a dad to tell your son about God. He is the strong third strand in your rope, intertwined invisibly with the two of you. And as we discussed earlier, you are his first human impression of what his Creator is like. Showing your son who the Lord is, though, can be done in many ways. Here's how God originally instructed parents to tell their kids about Him:

> Love the LORD your God with all your heart and with all your soul and with all your strength. These commandments that I give you today are to be upon your hearts. Impress them on your children. Talk about them when you sit at home and when you walk along the road, when you lie down and when you get up. Tie them as symbols on your hands and bind them on your foreheads. Write them on the doorframes of your houses and on your gates. (Deut. 6:5–9)

Unfortunately, we are experts at *segmenting* our Christianity, meaning we divide our interaction with God into parts: quiet times, church services, Bible studies, family prayer time. But from the very beginning, God never intended our relationship with Him to look like slices of a pie, cut up into separate spiritual parts. Instead, He desires a more natural approach. A more natural, instinctive, non-artificial relationship. He wants the way we communicate faith in the home to be more holistic. And the great news is that you can custom-fit that to your own personality and family dynamic. This is the best way to impress the things of God onto our children.

When you sit at home . . . when you lie down: Early on in your son's development, you have some unique opportunities to be with him. Take bedtime. A perfect chance to talk to your son about God just before he closes his eyes at night. This was one way we began introducing our sons to Jesus. We developed a nightly habit of reading short and well-illustrated Bible story books to them. These stories opened their minds and imaginations to God's creative and redemptive work throughout history. We read other spiritual stories to them as well.

We also began praying together. Not big-people prayers, but short, simple ones that centered on basic truths about God. And our requests targeted kid stuff. We didn't burden them with world issues or matters interesting to adults. We prayed about the dog, our pet bird, family-related and personal concerns. We wanted their young minds to know they could talk to God about anything at anytime, and that if it's important to them, then it's important to God (see Phil. 4:6–7; 1 Peter 5:7). We also used bedtime to begin memorizing short Scripture verses together.

All this took virtually zero preparation on my part. I just showed up at bedtime, loved on my boys, and directed their thoughts toward God. As they grew older, we used devotion books and Christian biographies as well. But my wife and I made sure we avoided lecturing, never preached at them and always tried to be interesting. And the best times we ever had were the ones when they talked more than we did.

Of course, the bedtime dynamic changes. It did for us. And your son probably won't respond as well to you sitting on the edge of his bed as he grows older. Just be sensitive to this and be willing to flex and transition.

When you walk along the road: But the greatest, and often most meaningful times we've had with our boys have always happened while we were simply living out our daily lives. Those moments have come as an overflow—unplanned, freestyle, ad-libbing the faith. From within. Out of the abundance in our hearts. And this is also the way God intends it to be. The door of a kid's heart opens and closes randomly and quickly, without warning. Closed, not out of rebellion, but closed in the sense that his interests and attention can change from minute to minute. These "open" life moments are golden opportunities to impress our kids with God's reality. For His relevance to have an impact on them. To impart to them something about life and how God relates to it. It's a chance to demonstrate to them that God is more than a churchy, religious, abstract concept, but instead a real heavenly Father who intersects and lives in everyday life.

You'll find as your boy grows older, these informal times will far outweigh anything you might plan. They're, in fact, the norm. The rule, not the exception. And they're just as ordained by God as any organized or planned time. God works in everyday life, not just when we schedule Him in. And that's exactly what you want—for spiritual discussion in your father-son relationship to be as natural as playing catch or fishing or watching a movie together.

Relating spiritually to your son in a natural way communicates that God is as real and relevant as anything else in his life . . . even more so! It protects him from the danger of segmenting or compartmentalizing his spiritual life. Through natural communication, he'll see that God is a part of everything, not just the "spiritual" areas. We don't need to turn every conversation into some spiritual observation or lesson. We need to resist the temptation to "teach" and instead help our sons see every good thing in life as coming from God (see James 1:17). This turns the lyrics of Christianity into live music, with melody, harmony, and a kicking beat, too!

The truth is, your son will catch more of what faith in God is really like simply from being around you. His relationship with you is his greatest asset in his faith development. And it's your most effective tool in passing on that faith to him. Read the last two sentences again.

Sometimes when I travel, I get to take my family with me. One time while I was speaking at a beach retreat, I rented a WaveRunner and took the family out for a spin. After jumping some waves at full speed and scaring my wife half to death, I returned to shore and picked up all three boys. We raced out onto the open water, leaving the beach as fast as we could, jumping waves, laughing, and hanging on tightly to each other. As guys, we wanted to see how fast the thing could go. So I "floored it." And right as we were about to reach top speed, we looked to our right and spotted an entire school of dolphins swimming beside us. Swimming beside us! We were all amazed at the sight. We raced them for a while, then slowed down as the seven or eight dolphins disappeared under the water and swam away. I turned the engine off and just savored the moment while we caught our breath. There we were, soaked head to toe with the tang of saltwater in our mouths.

"Hey guys," I said, "who'd like to thank God for the dolphins?"

One of the boys volunteered a quick prayer, right there out on the ocean, and then we were off again for some more wave jumping. It wasn't awkward or forced. But neither was it expected. It was just a part of life as we know it. It's still that way today. It's our thanking God for a mountaintop view. Bringing Him into the discussion while sharing an ice cold drink after working in the yard, riding home from a ballgame, or while making a sandwich in the kitchen. Or like a few nights ago, while sitting out under a crystal clear Texas sky with my nineteen-year-old. Staring at the stars together, God's heavenly handiwork sparked a number of deep conversations about the very deep intellect, creativity, and glory of our great God. We were there for hours.

Those times feel so right because they're so *natural*. Wherever and whenever, God is there, and welcome into our lives and relationships. Never forced, but filling every moment, even the silent ones. In that way, God is everywhere, and there is nowhere He is not relevant. And in that way my boys and I have the freedom to talk and pray about life without any pressure to act religious.

Our goal as parents has always been to reach the point in the relationship with our boys where talking about God, theology, prayer, the

Bible, world issues, or personal problems will become as natural and easy as "pass the salt, please."

In reality, you don't have to be an expert on the Bible to make God that important third strand in your relationship. It only matters that you're growing and processing your own relationship with your heavenly Father. My kids frankly couldn't care less that their dad has a Master's of Theology degree, spent decades teaching the Scripture, and has written a bunch of books. Big deal. Don't get me wrong. They're proud of me, of course, and of what I've accomplished. But all they ultimately care about is that I am real, loving, and authentic.

They just want me to be their dad.

Father Figures

As Dad, you're the number-one guy in your son's life, but parenting is still a team sport. Mom has a massive role as well. But as great as his parents' ministry is in his life, your son nevertheless needs other men in his life who model for him manhood and faith. As dads, we need the support and influence of those outside the home because our sons eventually spend lots of time away from home and our direct influence. That's why, when you find people and ministries that complement the spiritual vision you have for your children, you should partner with them. And in a big way. You're all in this thing together when you allow others to supplement what you're doing in your son's life.

Often God will take an area of your son's life where you've planted and watered and use another man to cause growth in that area. That's why kids sometimes listen to someone else who says the same thing you've been saying for years! But don't be discouraged or jealous. This simply lets you know that your efforts in his life have not been in vain. For many years I, as a youth minister, have been that "someone else" to dads, but now I'm enjoying the benefits of having other men model and speak into my own sons' lives.

Team sport, remember?

So support your church and its youth group or some other youth ministry where your son is mentored. Scout leaders, coaches, teachers, church leaders, and older Christian boys can all play a part in mentoring your son.

Being a dad is a job that's bigger than all of us. It requires the wisdom of Solomon, the strength of Samson, and the patience of Job! It's a God-sized task. That's why we need all the support we can get—other men who share similar values. We want to surround our kids with men and expose them to adults who will help contribute to their development as followers of God. And if you have some of these men currently in your son's life, thank them. Tell them what a strategic role they're playing. Encourage them. Reward them if you can.

Fruit

So how can you know if your son is starting to grasp this baton of faith? How can you be sure that he's even interested? What are the outer "signs of life" that tell you something is actually happening on the inside? It's easy to become discouraged because we may not see anything significant happening in our kids' lives. But often this can be due to poor eyesight on our part. There may actually be more spiritual fruit than we realize.

I'm a slow learner, but experience has taught me that young people are capable of growth and maturity, just like adults. They can handle deep truth and accomplish great things for God. Adults, though, often under-challenge or misunderstand kids.

Sometimes we can be quite unfair to kids concerning this whole "bearing fruit" thing, expecting them to look and act like little adults. We also forget that when it comes to maturity, God's work is always done over time. And even the healthiest trees go through times when they bear little or no fruit. But that doesn't mean the tree is dead, dying, or unhealthy. Further, during some seasons trees bear more fruit than during others. But isn't this also true of adult Christians? And kid fruit or teenage fruit doesn't always look just like our adult fruit. Nor should it. When you took your son to the doctor for his six-month checkup, for example, your physician examined him to look for signs of healthy baby growth, not healthy adult development. Fruit is most often age appropriate, and relates to the growth of each individual according to where they are in their spiritual development. This is the way that God works in us. That's why the men's ministry and the children's ministry meet separately! Kid fruit might include:

- Showing initial interest in spiritual things
- Expressing a desire to attend a youth group or student ministry
- Developing healthy friendships with other teenagers
- Doing what you ask without arguing or talking back
- Saying "please," "thank you," "may I?" or "yes, sir"
- Volunteering to pray, but doing it his way, in a comfortable language
- Reading his Bible on his own
- Asking challenging questions about God or the Bible
- Choosing on his own to say no to a questionable social activity
- Making unprompted comments about God or spiritual issues

As dads, our job is to be on the lookout for spiritual fruit in any of its many forms and to praise our boys for it. This kind of encouragement goes a long way at this stage of life when most comments they hear are put-downs. They need to know that somebody believes in them, that somebody is cheering for them.

Nothing Is Sacred; Everything Is Sacred

We touched on this earlier, but I'm reinforcing it here because I think we so easily lose the concept: If your boy is to embrace that faith you've been telling him about, then he'll need to be convinced that all of life is a gift from God, not just the "religious" parts. You have to show him that all of life is to be enjoyed, and that it all comes from Him. It means that you find a way, verbally or nonverbally, to give God credit for all the good stuff in life—sports, music, food, and fun! I've always wanted my boys to see God as One who loves, lives, and laughs. When you have fun with your son, you're teaching him that God is fun and the Christian life is meant to be enjoyed, not merely endured. Communicating faith this way, I've painted a backdrop that has contributed to my effectiveness in passing on Christianity to my kids.

But though I am, by profession, a communicator, I believe I've taught my sons more about faith in God not by what I've said but by what I've done. Like the time I told the grocery store clerk that he gave me back too much change. That said something about God to my sons. Or the time I yelled at one of my boys and had to ask him to forgive me. Or maybe my humble and controlled response to the man at church who verbally attacked me one day. Or perhaps when my sons have seen me endure hardship as a church planter, or trust God for our finances. Or it could have been the way I've told them every day how much I love them and how great I think they are.

I've enjoyed my faith. My boys know I don't care for negative, legalistic rituals and rules. They know that I hate the idea of being religious, but I love the reality of being authentic with God. We laugh a lot in the Kinley house, even during some really hard times. I've been honest with my sons when I've had no answers from God, and been real in sharing how He is, in many ways, a big mystery to me. We've come to believe as a family that faith in God is more than an event. It's more often than not a *process*—a long and bloody one. And though this pursuit of Christ isn't always seamless and pristine, my boys know by the way I act and relate that walking with God is the most dynamic, wonderful, risky, painful, and fun thing a real man could ever do.

And through it all I sense their grip tightening on that baton a little every day.

So, dads, don't be discouraged. Don't ever give up hope for your sons and their faith. Do for them what you know you need to do. But more importantly, be the man you need to be before God. Be yourself. And as much as it's in your power, keep the bond between you and your boy strong. Grip that baton. Extend it to your son. Remember those who took the time and made the sacrifice to pass it on to you. Look ahead in your lane. See your son there with his hand extended toward you, waiting for you to place the greatest treasure in life firmly into his grasp. Then take a deep breath of faith, reaching deep inside yourself . . . and run!

CHAPTER 10

Letting Go

Those eminent theologians, the Rolling Stones, once wrote, "Time waits for no man, and it won't wait for me."[1] That's not just classic rock and roll or good theology. It's practical wisdom too. Time does indeed march on. Relentlessly. Like a soldier on a mission. Time has a job to do, a destiny to fulfill. Racing toward ultimate extinction in eternity, it cannot be slowed or stopped, only measured, harnessed, redeemed, and used. Solomon said, "There is a time for everything . . . a time to plant and a time to uproot" (Eccl. 3:1–2). I'm not convinced one of history's wisest men was talking about parenting here, but I'm pretty sure he would agree that there is also a time for *letting go*. A time when a dad's grip on his son loosens, relinquishing the strong guidance and direct influence he once had. Granted, that day may seem light-years away right now, but it will inevitably come. And it's your job to prepare your son, and yourself, for that day. Even today is one tick of life's clock closer to the time when you'll close an important chapter in your father-son relationship. An end to an epic era of life for you and him.

Dad, before we know it, it's time to release our sons. A time to say goodbye. It's a gut-wrenching episode of parenting, and ironically, one for which we have striven all these years. The whole reason we've exerted an enormous amount of time, energy, money, sacrifice, and investment is just so that we could arrive at this day with confidence.

Hard to imagine? I understand. The future always is. Those now blank pages of life's journal are difficult to visualize as fully written in our minds. But once again, here's where that vision we discussed in chapter 2 comes into play. You've spent all this time preparing him. And you desperately hope that on that day he'll be ready to face college, the workforce, and whatever life may throw at him. You hope he's ready to stand on his own. To be a man in a world that will assuredly challenge his spirituality and manhood. To respond to the call of character when tested. To take the lessons of love and compassion he has learned while living under your roof and apply them to his future relationships at college, on the job, and ultimately with a wife and family of his own. You pray that the faith and love for God you have so diligently deposited in him over the years will continue to be his compass, his well, and his rock. Like tributaries into a river, all the hopes and dreams you once had for him converge during this climactic season of life.

Some dads let go too soon. At the first sign of independence or rebellion in their sons, they respond with the extremes of either backing off or administering a harsh, heavy dose of "tough love." But that's the "quick-fix" mentality, and it doesn't work very well on the heart. Too much discipline too soon can damage your relationship with him. Giving your son too much freedom or responsibility too early can hinder his chances of developing into manhood. Allowing him to experience too much independence before he is able to handle it will prematurely communicate that he is ready to make the break with dad. Self-reliance is a good thing, but granted too soon can result in more harm than good. In reality, letting go isn't an event, but rather a process. A long one. It begins incrementally early on in his life. As he grows and matures, you allow him more independence, decision-making, freedom to choose, and freedom to fail.

When I taught Clayton to ride a bike, we were at the beach renting a house on North Carolina's beautiful Outer Banks during a much-deserved sabbatical from pastoring. Just a short distance from where the Wright brothers first took flight and changed the world forever, we spent a month sightseeing, climbing lighthouses, crabbing, and taking long walks on the beach. So with all this free time, we had brought along our bikes in hopes of exploring the area. It was the perfect opportunity to finally teach my son to ride a bike. So after securely setting the training wheels, Clayton pedaled as expected, with no problems other than a few steering glitches. But once I took those wheels off, that's when things got interesting. Of course I held his seat and jogged with him down the long paved driveway until he seemed to get the hang of it. And then I did it.

I let go.

Slowing my jog down to a walk, I eventually stopped and watched nervously as he pedaled forward . . . and headfirst into a bush! Scratched, bleeding, and with a slight ego bruise, Clayton picked himself up. I ran over, turned his bike around and set him off again back down the driveway. And after a few attempts, he finally got the hang of it, without any more help from dad. But though it was many years ago, I still remember what it felt like to let go of that bicycle, wondering to myself if he would instantly plow face-first into the pavement. I envisioned busted lips and broken teeth. But following that initial bush incident, we were soon cruising the Outer Banks in style.

Of course, as you look back over the years, there's always room for second-guessing and self-criticism. *I should have . . .* or *I wish I had done more . . .* or *Why didn't I . . . ?*

Maybe so. But hey, every dad has those thoughts. More than anything though, you just want to work hard and do your best before God. That's all any of us can do. We have to trust Him to do the rest. Our boys are growing into men, physically. That's a given. But it's our mission to help them grow toward *complete* manhood—emotionally, relationally, mentally, and spiritually. And our prayer is that they would continue to grow in those areas long after leaving home. Some of that is determined by your investment in him while you had him. The rest of it is determined by the choices he will make on his own after he is gone. But for this to happen, at some point you have to take the training wheels off. You have to let him go.

So how can you turn this heavy page of life's book and one day transition into this new, unknown chapter of fatherhood?

To begin with, I think it's a healthy exercise to think back and remember the years you've had with your son. God gave you the gift of *memory* so you can recall the good times and experiences you had with your boy. This helps you regain some perspective as you face the time of letting him go. God gives you a son for just a little while, and then you have to give him back. It's a long stewardship really, and one that in retrospect passes all too quickly. But it's a healthy exercise to replay the highlight film in your mind, remembering him as a baby, and all those dreams you had for him. Those memories call to mind the emotions you felt the first time you saw him. Maybe those familiar tears will well up in your eyes again. Maybe one will even escape, cascading down your cheek (just pretend you're having a contact lens issue). Seriously though, don't ever be afraid to get emotional about your boy. A dad *should* get sentimental about his son, and often. We need more sentimental dads. It proves the relationship touches the most tender spot of your heart. If Jesus got emotional over people He loved, then surely you have permission to do the same (see Luke 13:34; John 11:35).

Now close your eyes and envision that highlight film for a minute. Can you see your boy taking his first steps? That first toothless grin? His T-ball games? Do you recall all those times you wrestled on the floor? The good old days when you were "Superman" to him? The movies you watched and the popcorn you shared? The burgers you consumed? The fish you caught? The hikes you made? The hunting trips you took? The projects you shared? Those family vacations? And the memories that flood your mind are like a multicolored collage of unimaginable joy. Then you're suddenly hit with the overwhelming awareness that God must really, really love you. And you shake your head in wonder and whisper to yourself, *Wow, I had a son.*

What an incredible, mind-blowing privilege. And know this, dad. No one can ever rob you of those memories made and times spent enjoying life with your son. They belong to you forever. The heartache comes when dads arrive at this time of life only to realize they didn't do what was necessary to *make* those memories.

Don't be that guy.

Right now you have a choice to make every day special with your son. Don't let work, laziness, or your own sense of inadequacy steal that from you. Yes, it's a man-sized challenge, a *dad-sized* challenge, and one like no other any of us have ever faced. But you can do it! You can!

And yet even as you read these words, that day draws near. Galloping like a black stallion toward the gates of your castle. When it's all said and done, you will have spent almost two decades laboring. Straining. Struggling. Sacrificing. Giving. Praying. Leading. Sharing. *Fathering.*

And there is no higher calling in this life.

None.

Train Whistles

There's an old Norman Rockwell painting that's especially meaningful to me. It's called *Breaking Home Ties*, and it was discovered years ago hidden behind a wall in Rockwell's Vermont home. In it, Rockwell depicts a dad's final moments with his son before he leaves home. The father and son are sitting on the running board of an old 1930s truck. The dad is obviously a farmer, dressed in well-worn jeans, a wrinkled denim shirt with the sleeves rolled up, and black boots. His sun-baked hands clutch two hats—one his old, dusty field hat and the other, a newer one he holds for his son. A homemade cigarette dangles from his mouth. His hair has grayed around the temples. On his face are crevices carved from age and years of hard work. He's leaning over, waiting for the sound of a train whistle, a sound that will signal the lump to form in his throat. There's a slight hint of worry on his brow. Or perhaps he's just thinking about what he's going to say to his boy when the conductor shouts, "All aboard!" Then comes that moment when he looks his son squarely in the eyes and says his goodbye.

The boy, on the other hand, is sitting erect and in excited expectation. His brows are raised as he peers down the road in anticipation of the train that is soon to arrive. He's dressed for the journey in his Sunday suit, complete with crooked tie. Cradled gently in his hands is a lunch wrapped in paper, no doubt prepared one last time by a loving and thoughtful mom. And I bet there's a note slipped inside. His bags are all packed, complete with a college pennant sticker already stuck on the side of his suitcase. On top of that suitcase sit three books, portraying his enthusiasm to dive into college life. On his knee rests the head of the family dog, a loyal collie with a forlorn look in his eyes. But the boy is ready, eager for what lies ahead and for what life has in store for him.

This dad looks like he's at the end of a long journey. He's given it all he had. Now together, he and his son sit in silence. Not a word spoken between them. One reflecting. The other anticipating. One remembering. The other waiting. The time for speeches has long since passed. Appropriately named by Rockwell, those *Home Ties* are indeed in the process of being broken in this scene. It's time.

Time to let go.

Friend, one day you will arrive at this same inevitable intersection. A place in your parental journey when you will symbolically walk your son to the edge of the driveway. You will accompany him to the airport or deposit him onto some college campus teeming with undisciplined teenagers. At the very least he will leave the home he has known and loved all these years, poised and ready for the next chapter in his life. As for me, I have been hearing train whistles for months now.

Ever since ninth grade, my oldest son has felt a calling on his life to enter some sort of law enforcement or military career. As time went on, he began to sense God was calling him to attend the United States Military Academy at West Point, the prestigious college famous for producing great leaders like Robert E. Lee, Ulysses S. Grant, Douglas MacArthur, George Patton, Dwight Eisenhower, and Norman Schwarzkopf. Presidents, governors, astronauts, heads of state, and military leaders have all graduated from this famous academy. It's where teenagers are molded into soldiers and trained to be officers and leaders, prepared to defend the sovereignty of the United States of America. West Point takes only those young men and women whom they firmly believe to be America's best young leaders, athletes, and students. Of the 10,000 who apply each year, only some 3,700 receive the required Congressional nominations. In a highly competitive process, about 1,300 are extended invitations to become cadets at the world's greatest military academy.

Last fall, U.S. Senator Mark Pryor called us late one night from his Washington office to inform us that Clayton was among those selected and invited to attend West Point. For Clayton, this marked the beginning of a dream come true. And thus began the start of an exciting adventure and potential career as an officer in the United States Army. It also represents a full scholarship worth some $475,000!

But for Beverly and me, West Point means something much more. Beyond scholarship money and the quality of education he'll receive, we also recognize it as a perfect fit for our son. For years, it's been clear to us that Clayton's desire and destiny lie in protecting freedom and liberating the oppressed. His growth of character and well roundedness has made him who he is today. Just a few weeks prior to writing these words, our family made the long trip from Little Rock, Arkansas, to West Point, New York. After a few days spent playing in New York City (this time we had GPS in the car!), we made the hour-and-a-half drive north to West Point where we spent the night in a local hotel. That evening, we sat on our beds as I read a tribute to Clayton while his mom and two younger brothers listened. I'd been writing this thing for months. And for months, I'd felt like that old farmer in Rockwell's painting. Counting down the days. Waiting for that awful, glorious moment.

We'd spent some really good times together during his senior year. But most were spent just doing ordinary things, like riding in the car or sitting at the kitchen counter. Or just sitting on the front porch at night engaged in deep conversation. But, honestly, the best part was just being together.

Father and son.

And so, on that last night, I simply praised my son for the honorable life he's lived. He's heard me say lots of those things before. Words and emotions I've shared with him from childhood up to now. But this time it was different. Knowing he'll be some 1,300 miles away and only able to come home a couple of times a year, this was my opportunity to tell Clayton just what he means to me. More than anything, I wanted him to know one more time how proud I am of him. I wanted him to understand in a fresh way how he has brought my heart such inexpressible joy. I wanted him to know he has run a good race thus far, and that we would support him every day in prayer as he faces the huge challenge ahead of him. I formally gave him my blessing, not just for the path he has chosen, but more so for the *man* he had become. It was . . . er . . . an emotional time.

And I heard that train whistle off in the distance.

The next morning we stood outdoors in line for a few hours. We could see the Hudson River flowing in the distance. It was a hot, beautiful Monday morning. Finally, it was our turn, and they ushered forty-four prospective new cadets and their families into Eisenhower Auditorium. It was easy to spot the nervous and anxious looks on the other hundred or so parents and siblings. I listened intently as an Army officer confidently stepped up to the podium. "*Candidates, congratulations on your acceptance to the United States Military Academy at West Point. You wouldn't be here unless we thought you have what it takes to become an Army officer. The next forty-seven months will be intense, I promise you. But the rewards will far outweigh the sacrifice. Specifically, the next six weeks of Cadet Basic Training will be grueling. But believe in yourself and keep a positive attitude. Others have walked the same path before you and survived. You will as well.*"

I glanced across the aisle at Clayton. His hands gripped a small black duffle bag that rested in his lap, just like the young man in the Rockwell painting. I could tell he was listening intently to every word that came from the man in the green uniform. After months of prayer and preparation, I couldn't believe we were finally there. As Clayton listened intently, I couldn't take my eyes off him. An ocean wave of pride and emotion swept over me, and I thought for a second I might lose it.

Not that anyone would notice. Dads all over the auditorium were fighting back the same emotions. Some were welling up with tears. Moms were already wiping their eyes. But my private moment was suddenly interrupted as my thoughts jolted back to the man at the podium. He finished his remarks, and then another officer stepped forward to the microphone.

"At this time, parents and families please say your goodbyes. You have ninety seconds."

That announcement reverberated like a canon shot to the heart of every dad there that day.

Ninety seconds. One and a half minutes to compress nineteen years of life and relationship. Almost two decades now reduced to a few seconds of goodbye. After his brothers and mom had said their abbreviated farewells, it was my turn. Earlier in the trip I had invoked the rite of "last hug," proving that there are still a few perks left for dad. Then my son and I enjoyed a strong embrace. The kind men give each other. I can only describe it as epic. My boys and I have always loved to hug.

It didn't last long, but just long enough to communicate deep love, mutual respect, and the strong-as-steel bond that exists between us. And during those few seconds, my thoughts were flooded with the huge challenge that lay ahead of my boy. How his mind, body, character, courage, and spirit would be severely tested in the months to come. I could now clearly hear that train conductor in my mind, issuing his final call,

ALL ABOARD!

And just before my son picked up his bag and assumed his spot in line, I placed my hand firmly against his chest, looked him squarely in the eyes, and whispered in a slightly quivering voice, "Clayton, everything you need to succeed is right in here."

With humble confidence, I knew I had given him everything I had. It was time for him to go. He acknowledged my comment by nodding his head in classic Clayton style. And with that, I watched him walk out the auditorium door and into a whole new life.

The arrow had officially left the bow.

My first dad-sized challenge was complete.

And my grip relaxed and released as I committed him into another Father's hands.

Later that afternoon, Clayton, dressed now in uniform and with head shaved in military style, stood at attention with 1,300 other future Army officers. Raising his right hand, he took a solemn oath to support the Constitution and defend our great country. And as they marched off, we caught one final, brief glimpse of him. I couldn't help myself and shouted "Go Kinley!"

I am such a dork.

Or maybe I'm just a very proud dad. Though I have loved this boy with all my heart since before he was born, there is One who loves him infinitely more than I do, and who has invested much more than I have in him. His sacrifice is greater than any I could make on this earth. My sons belong to God. And though my boys have done a lot of growing up since the day they first came screaming into this world, so have I. Truthfully, I have a lot more growing to do, and quite a ways to go in my own personal journey of manhood. While Clayton is in the process of joining the Long Gray Line, his dad is still in the long, bloody process of becoming who my Lord wants me to be. The work is still going on within me (see Phil. 1:6).

Thank God.

The Real Deal

Throughout this book I have hesitated to try and define manhood for you. The definitions the so-called "experts" give seem boring, unattainable, and one-dimensional to me. Because of this, I have refrained from providing concrete descriptions, such as "Real men are . . ." or "Manhood is . . ." I just didn't want to give the impression that all men should look the same. They shouldn't. Or that if you failed to reach some super-spiritual level of personal achievement, you were somehow deficient in your masculinity or progress toward manhood. Instead, I'll let God fill in those blanks and continue making you into the man you are to be. So in lieu of a single definition of the "Christian man," perhaps a multidimensional portrait of manhood has slowly emerged out of the pages of this book as we have discussed the rugged adventure of the father-son relationship. In an ironic sort of way, *we* learn to become men, in part by showing our sons how to do the same.

But as you anticipate this climactic chapter of fatherhood, please don't dread it. Sure, it's a season of loss, but it's also the celebration and culmination of a very big win. In fact, your son's leaving home may be your finest hour so far. It was for me.

King David, meditating on this, wrote the following words:

> Unless the Lord builds the house, its builders labor in vain. Unless the Lord watches over the city, the watchmen stand guard in vain. In vain you rise early and stay up late, toiling for food to eat—for he grants sleep to those he loves. Sons are a heritage from the Lord, children a reward from him. *Like arrows in the hands of a warrior are sons born in one's youth.* Blessed is the man whose quiver is full of them. They will not be put to shame when they contend with their enemies in the gate. (Ps. 127:1–5, emphasis added)

For the whole fatherhood experience to be worth it, I think God has to be in it in a big way. From start to finish, and at every point along the way. At the end of our lives, when we find ourselves dying in a hospital bed or tottering around some city park with a cane, it won't matter how much money we made. It will only matter *who* we made. What we did in this life won't mean anything unless our primary mission was to be the best dads we could be. Sons are a *heritage* from the Lord. Wow! Think about that statement! Do you see your son as a rich heritage, bequeathed from God Himself to you? Like a world treasure? An inheritance straight from heaven? A reward from your Father? Is your son like a mighty arrow in your hands, drawn back, aimed, and prepared to one day pass on a legacy of his own? How happy is the man who has a son!

So how happy are you? Are you finding some of life's greatest pleasure and reward in being a dad to your son? If so, then keep at it. Stay the course. And if not, considering what's at stake, what choices will you make to change that?

I hope this book has inspired you to pursue real relationship with your son. To strengthen the beautiful, manly bond that began the moment he came into your life. That, above all, is the point. What our nation and world desperately need are men who will dedicate their lives to this high calling of fatherhood. Nobody else can ever be what you are to your son. Nobody. So dad, don't bail on him. Don't coast on yesterday's wins and don't get sidetracked by past failures. Don't give up during the tough times and don't fear the future. With God's help, you'll outlast those hard times and overcome the uncertainty of the days ahead. Focus instead on being God's man for your boy! This will be the greatest thing you ever do.

Finally, I trust this book has challenged you, man-to-man, in the relentless pursuit of fatherhood. A challenge to channel that passion you have for your boy into influencing your own choices. To obey that thirst within your soul, crying out in desperation to raise your son to authentic manhood. Isn't that what you really want? And wouldn't you be willing to separate yourself from anything that threatens this destiny of yours? Would you pause and beg God *right now* to help you to be the man your son deserves? Will you daily choose to demonstrate to your boy that he is the *best part* of your life? And would you put this book down right now and go tell him what a treasure he is to you? Hey dad, it's up to you. The clock is ticking. It's game time. *Your* time.

Go and build your great tower!

To learn more about Jeff Kinley and Main Thing Ministries, visit http://www.mainthingministries.com/.

Notes

Chapter 8: Taming the Lion

1. Jerry Ropelato, "Internet Pornography Statistics," http://internet-filter-review.toptenreviews.com/internet-pornography-statistics.html.

Chapter 10: Letting Go

1. Mick Jagger and Keith Richards, "Time Waits for No One," *It's Only Rock 'N Roll*, released October 18, 1974, ℗ Promotone B. V. under exclusive license to Universal International Music.